Shelley's Ghost

Shelley's Ghost

RESHAPING THE IMAGE OF A LITERARY FAMILY

Stephen Hebron and Elizabeth C. Denlinger

Bodleian Library
UNIVERSITY OF OXFORD

First published in 2010 by the Bodleian Library
Broad Street
Oxford OX1 3BG

www.bodleianbookshop.co.uk

ISBN 978 1 85124 339 6

Designed by Dot Little
Typeset in Monotype Baskerville 10.5 on 14 pt body text, with display headings in 17 pt.
Printed and bound by Great Wall Printing, China
British Library Catalogue in Publishing Data
A CIP record of this publication is available from the British Library

Contents

Acknowledgements

From New York Public Library I would like to thank Lailani Courtney and Susan Rabbiner, and from Dove Cottage Michael McGregor, Jeff Cowton and Jane Connolly.

I have received a great deal of friendly support at the Bodleian Libraries, and must thank in particular Richard Ovenden, Theodora Boorman, Samuel Fanous, Michael Hughes, Caroline Brooke Johnson, Dot Little, Charlotte Mckillop-Mash, Robert Minte, Judith Priestman, Madeline Slaven, and Deborah Susman.

I am especially grateful to Bruce Barker-Benfield, Liz Denlinger, Chris Fletcher and John and Virginia Murray.

Stephen Hebron

Joint Directors' foreword

The two greatest collections of manuscripts and rare books relating to the poet Percy Bysshe Shelley and his circle are in the Bodleian Libraries, Oxford, and The New York Public Library. The Bodleian collection comprises the family papers of Shelley, his wife Mary Wollstonecraft Shelley, and Mary's parents, William Godwin and Mary Wollstonecraft. The collection in New York was the creation of the financier Carl H. Pforzheimer, Sr., who took a special interest in the lives and works of Shelley and his contemporaries. It was developed by his descendants, and in 1986 the Carl and Lily Pforzheimer Foundation donated the Shelley and His Circle Collection to The New York Public Library.

Two-thirds of the Shelley family papers came to the Bodleian through gifts and bequest between 1893 and 1961. The remaining portion was inherited by the Barons Abinger. Between 1974 and 1993 the 8th Lord Abinger deposited almost all the papers at the Bodleian Libraries on long-term loan. In 2004, following an international appeal, the Bodleian purchased the papers from the 9th Lord Abinger.

The purchase of the Abinger Papers has enabled them to be fully catalogued for the first time. It has also provided the occasion for the publication of this book, and for major exhibitions in Oxford and New York. In 2010–11 the Bodleian Shelley collection will be on display in Oxford, together, for the first time, with some of the greatest treasures in the Pforzheimer collection. In 2011–12 significant parts of the Bodleian collection will be on show first at Dove Cottage, Grasmere, and then in The New York Public Library.

This project is the latest example of the continuing fruitful relationship between the Bodleian and The New York Public Library. We are very grateful to all those on both sides of the Atlantic who have helped in its realization, and are particularly grateful to Carl H. Pforzheimer III, John and Virginia Murray, Dr Leonard Polonsky and John Koh of Bernard Quaritch Ltd for their guidance and support.

Sarah E. Thomas
Bodley's Librarian and Director of Bodleian Libraries

Paul LeClerc
President of The New York Public Library

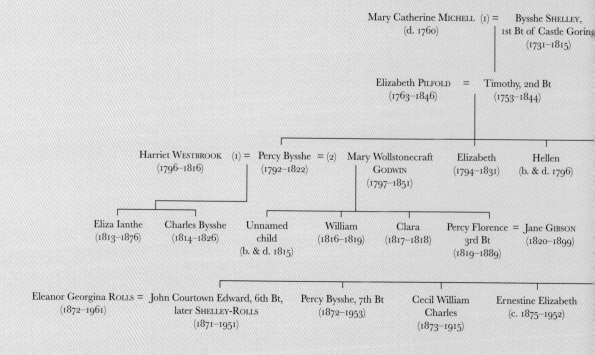

Mary Catherine MICHELL (1) = Bysshe SHELLEY,
(d. 1760)   1st Bt of Castle Goring
                             (1731–1815)

Elizabeth PILFOLD = Timothy, 2nd Bt
(1763–1846)   (1753–1844)

Harriet WESTBROOK (1) = Percy Bysshe = (2) Mary Wollstonecraft   Elizabeth   Hellen
(1796–1816)   (1792–1822)   GODWIN   (1794–1831)   (b. & d. 1796)
                                          (1797–1851)

Eliza Ianthe   Charles Bysshe   Unnamed   William   Clara   Percy Florence = Jane GIBSON
(1813–1876)   (1814–1826)   child   (1816–1819)   (1817–1818) 3rd Bt   (1820–1899)
                                  (b. & d. 1815)   (1819–1889)

Eleanor Georgina ROLLS = John Courtown Edward, 6th Bt,   Percy Bysshe, 7th Bt   Cecil William   Ernestine Elizabeth
(1872–1961)   later SHELLEY-ROLLS   (1872–1953)   Charles   (c. 1875–1952)
                         (1871–1951)   (1873–1915)

The Shelley Baronetcy of Castle Goring

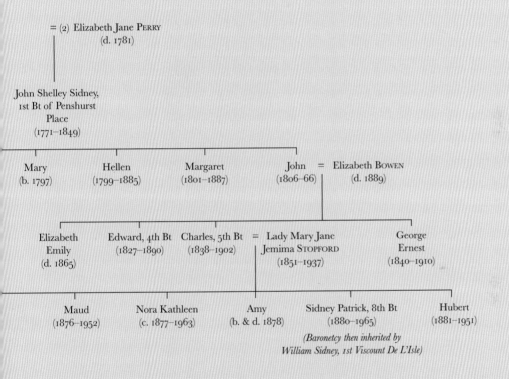

= (2) Elizabeth Jane PERRY
(d. 1781)

John Shelley Sidney,
1st Bt of Penshurst
Place
(1771–1849)

Mary
(b. 1797)

Hellen
(1799–1885)

Margaret
(1801–1887)

John   =   Elizabeth BOWEN
(1806–66)   (d. 1889)

Elizabeth
Emily
(d. 1865)

Edward, 4th Bt
(1827–1890)

Charles, 5th Bt   =   Lady Mary Jane
(1838–1902)   Jemima STOPFORD
(1851–1937)

George
Ernest
(1840–1910)

Maud
(1876–1952)

Nora Kathleen
(c. 1877–1963)

Amy
(b. & d. 1878)

Sidney Patrick, 8th Bt
(1880–1965)

Hubert
(1881–1951)

(Baronetcy then inherited by
William Sidney, 1st Viscount De L'Isle)

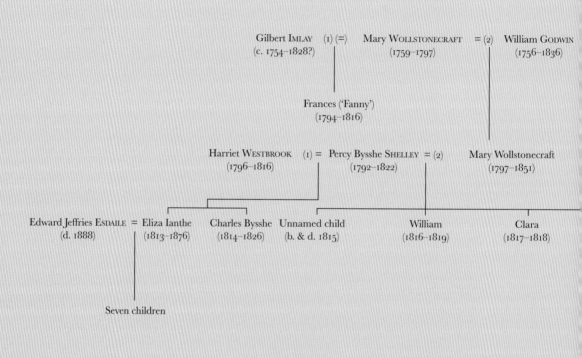

Gilbert IMLAY   (1) (=)   Mary WOLLSTONECRAFT   = (2)   William GODWIN
(c. 1754–1828?)   (1759–1797)   (1756–1836)

Frances ('Fanny')
(1794–1816)

Harriet WESTBROOK   (1) =   Percy Bysshe SHELLEY   = (2)   Mary Wollstonecraft
(1796–1816)   (1792–1822)   (1797–1851)

Edward Jeffries ESDAILE = Eliza Ianthe   Charles Bysshe   Unnamed child   William   Clara
(d. 1888)   (1813–1876)   (1814–1826)   (b. & d. 1815)   (1816–1819)   (1817–1818)

Seven children

Shelley Leopold Laurence,   Robert Brooke Campbell,   Hon. Lawrence
5th Baron ABINGER   6th Baron ABINGER   James Peter
(1872–1917)   (1876–1927)   (1877–1893)

The Shelley and Godwin Families

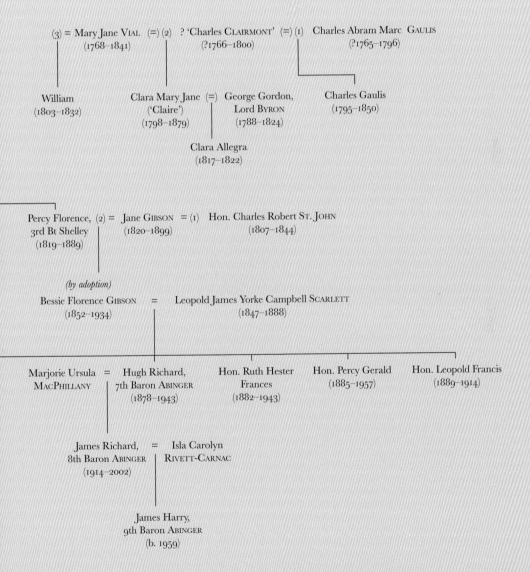

(3) = Mary Jane VIAL (=) (2) ? 'Charles CLAIRMONT' (=) (1) Charles Abram Marc GAULIS
      (1768–1841)   (?1766–1800)   (?1765–1796)

William
(1803–1832)

Clara Mary Jane (=) George Gordon,
('Claire')   Lord BYRON
(1798–1879)   (1788–1824)

Charles Gaulis
(1795–1850)

Clara Allegra
(1817–1822)

Percy Florence, (2) = Jane GIBSON = (1) Hon. Charles Robert ST. JOHN
3rd Bt Shelley   (1820–1899)   (1807–1844)
(1819–1889)

(by adoption)
Bessie Florence GIBSON   =   Leopold James Yorke Campbell SCARLETT
(1852–1934)   (1847–1888)

Marjorie Ursula = Hugh Richard,   Hon. Ruth Hester   Hon. Percy Gerald   Hon. Leopold Francis
MacPHILLANY   7th Baron ABINGER   Frances   (1885–1957)   (1889–1914)
                   (1878–1943)   (1882–1943)

James Richard,   =   Isla Carolyn
8th Baron ABINGER   RIVETT-CARNAC
(1914–2002)

James Harry,
9th Baron ABINGER
(b. 1959)

Preface

This book primarily tells the story of a remarkable family archive preserved in the Bodleian Library: the letters, journals and working papers of William Godwin and Mary Wollstonecraft, their daughter Mary, and Mary's husband Percy Bysshe Shelley. It is not a biography of these great literary figures, nor a critical appreciation of their work. Rather, it provides descriptions of, and quotations from, the manuscripts on which so many biographies and critical appreciations have been based, and explores how these manuscripts were either published or withheld by their owners in an attempt to shape the family's reputation.

The archive came to the Bodleian in three parts. Chapter 1 describes how the original gift was made in 1893. Chapter 2 explores how William Godwin gathered Mary Wollstonecraft's papers together after her death in 1797, and, controversially, exposed many of them to the public gaze. Chapter 3 focuses on the highly charged correspondence that flowed between Godwin, Shelley and Mary Shelley during the eight years of Shelley and Mary's marriage, and the trials and tragedies recorded therein. Chapters 4 and 5 look at what are perhaps the greatest treasures in the archive, the run of Shelley's working notebooks, and the original manuscript of Mary Shelley's novel *Frankenstein*. Chapters 6 and 7 trace how, after Shelley's sudden death in 1822, a grieving Mary collected and edited his work, and created a compelling image of his life and character. The penultimate chapter considers the efforts of the Shelleys' daughter-in-law, Jane, Lady Shelley, to control access to the archive, housed at the Shelley family home, Boscombe Manor in Dorset, and thereby shape, and establish once and for all, the family's public image. In it were preserved the family's literary endeavours and posthumous reputations; and after the writers' deaths the papers and relics embodied, like ghosts, their characters and lives.

Lady Shelley's efforts were bound to fail. Posterity, fascinated by highly unusual lives, and by literary work of exceptional quality, has investigated, scrutinized and judged. And the manuscripts have reflected, like prisms and mirrors, a plurality of images.

Not everything was preserved at Boscombe Manor and then presented to the Bodleian. Some manuscripts were given away, others were lost. Still more, belonging to family members and friends, fell into other hands. Elizabeth Denlinger's concluding chapter traces the fate of some of these scattered papers, and the motives of those collectors and scholars who so avidly pursued them.

Shelley and Oxford

An opening ceremony

On 14 June 1893 a ceremony was held at University College, Oxford. Among the assembled university dignitaries were the Rector of Exeter College, the President of Magdalen, the Wardens of Merton and All Souls, and the Master of Balliol. They had gathered to witness the opening of a memorial to one of the College's most celebrated former students, the poet Percy Bysshe Shelley. Representing the Shelley family that afternoon were the poet's grandson, William Esdaile, and Jane, Lady Shelley, the widow of the poet's son, Sir Percy Florence Shelley. Lady Shelley, a short, stout figure in her seventies, had commissioned the memorial, and now presented the Master of University College with a gold key. She thanked the college 'for enabling her to fulfil one of the dearest wishes of her heart'.[1] She had, she said, been a student of Shelley for more than forty years, and in that time had 'striven to give the world a just impression of his character'. She had been the companion of his son, and of his 'noble minded wife', Mary; she had known most of his friends, all of whom, she believed, were now dead. Those who fancied that Shelley and Mary had been 'regardless of the duties of life' were mistaken: 'Men of great genius could not always be reduced to rule. They erred sometimes, but they were not therefore to be deprived of the love and admiration of their countrymen.'

Lady Shelley's gold key gave access to a specially built chamber designed by the architect Basil Champneys. Short flights of steps led down to a domed space in which stood the Shelley monument: a statue in white marble of the poet, lying naked upon a sea-green marble slab and supported by an elaborate bronze pedestal. The statue, by Edward Onslow Ford, alluded to Shelley's fate: drowned, at the age of twenty-nine, off the Italian coast, his body washed up on a remote beach some days later. The bronze pedestal showed the muse of poetry seated between two winged lions.

Figure 1 The Shelley Memorial, University College, Oxford, by Edward Onslow Ford and Basil Champneys, opened in 1893. Photo: Richard Wheeler.

Figure 2 'The High
Street, Oxford', by
James Griffiths (1800).
The artist was Master
of University College,
(shown in the left of the
picture), when Shelley was
an undergraduate there.
Oxford, Bodleian Library,
G.A.Oxon a.86, fol. 49.

Figure 3 P.B. Shelley, *Poetical Essay on the Existing State of Things* (1811). Bernard Quaritch Ltd. The only known copy of this early pamphlet.

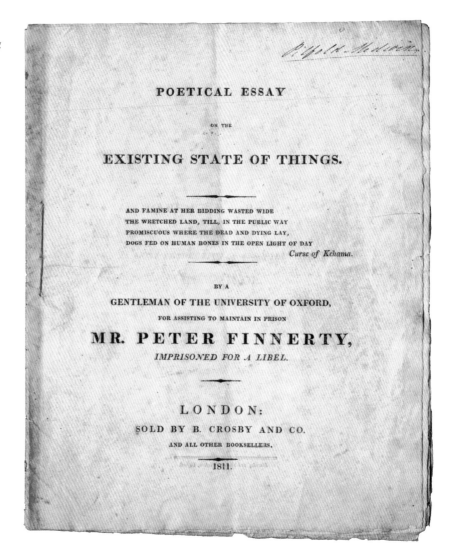

POETICAL ESSAY

ON THE

EXISTING STATE OF THINGS.

AND FAMINE AT HER BIDDING WASTED WIDE
THE WRETCHED LAND, TILL, IN THE PUBLIC WAY
PROMISCUOUS WHERE THE DEAD AND DYING LAY,
DOGS FED ON HUMAN BONES IN THE OPEN LIGHT OF DAY
Curse of Kehama.

BY A

GENTLEMAN OF THE UNIVERSITY OF OXFORD,

FOR ASSISTING TO MAINTAIN IN PRISON

MR. PETER FINNERTY,

IMPRISONED FOR A LIBEL.

LONDON:

SOLD BY B. CROSBY AND CO.

AND ALL OTHER BOOKSELLERS.

1811.

A gentleman of the University of Oxford

Oxford was not an obvious home for this striking memorial, for Shelley's university career had been brief and scandalous. As a schoolboy at Eton he had written a gothic romance, *Zastrozzi*. His father Timothy, a Sussex landowner of orthodox opinions, had, on bringing his son to Oxford in April or October 1810, called into Slatter & Munday, a printing and bookselling firm on the High Street, and according to Henry Slatter had said: 'My son here, has a literary turn, he is already an author; and do pray indulge him in his printing freaks'.[2] Shelley proceeded to publish, during his two terms at Oxford, 1810–11, a second gothic novel, *St. Irvyne; or, The Rosicrucian* (as 'A Gentleman of the University of Oxford'), and three radical pamphlets: first, a collection of verse jokingly titled *Posthumous Fragments of Margaret Nicholson; being Poems found amongst the*

Papers of that noted Female who attempted the Life of the King in 1786 (edited by one 'John Fitzvictor'); second, *Poetical Essay on the Existing State of Things*, supporting the Irish journalist Peter Finnerty, who had recently been imprisoned for slandering the Foreign Secretary, Lord Castlereagh; and third, *The Necessity of Atheism*, written anonymously with his great friend Thomas Jefferson Hogg. *The Necessity of Atheism*, was printed in Worthing, but Shelley personally laid out copies of it in Slatter & Munday's High Street window, for sale at sixpence each. There it was noticed by an appalled passing don, who demanded that the stock be burnt at the back of the shop. Subsequent enquiries established Shelley and Hogg as the authors, and when they refused to answer questions regarding it, or deny authorship, they were publicly expelled by University College.

'[H]ad the heads of the college been men of candid and broad intellects', Lady Shelley wrote reprovingly in 1859, 'they would have

Figure 4 P.B. Shelley and Thomas Jefferson Hogg, *The Necessity of Atheism* (1811). Oxford, Bodleian Library, Shelley e. 1(2).

12

considers it less probable that these men should have been deceived, than that the Deity should have appeared to them---our reason can never admit the testimony of men, who not only declare that they were eye-witnesses of miracles but that the Deity was irrational, for he commanded that he should be believed, he proposed the highest rewards for faith, eternal punishments for disbelief---we can only command voluntary actions, belief is not an act of volition, the mind is even passive, from this it is evident that we have not sufficient testimony,--or rather that testimony is insufficient to prove the being of a God, we have before shewn that it cannot be deduced from reason,---they who have been convinced by the evidence of the senses, they only can believe it.

From this it is evident that having no proofs from any of the three sources of conviction: the mind *cannot* believe the existence of a God, it is also evident that as belief is a passion of the

13

mind, no degree of criminality can be attached to disbelief, they only are reprehensible who willingly neglect to remove the false medium thro' which their mind views the subject.

It is almost unnecessary to observe, that the general knowledge of the deficiency of such proof, cannot be prejudicial to society : Truth has always been found to promote the best interests of mankind.---Every reflecting mind must allow that there is no proof of the existence of a Deity. Q. E. D.

Phillips, Printers, Worthing.

recognized in the author of the obnoxious pamphlet an earnest love of truth, a noble passion for arriving at the nature of things, however painful the road'.[3] She had originally intended to install Onslow Ford's monument not in Oxford, but over Shelley's grave in the non-Catholic Cemetery in Rome. She had dropped this idea, however, when the daughters of Shelley's friend Edward John Trelawny, whose grave lay next to the poet's, claimed ownership of that part of the cemetery. An alternative site was proposed to her in November 1891, when she received a letter from Professor Guido Biagi, Chief Librarian of the Biblioteca Medicea Laurenziana in Florence. Biagi had learned of Onslow Ford's statue, and of Lady Shelley's intention to present it 'to some public corporation'. He had, he told her, recently identified 'the precise spot where the body of the immortal poet was washed on shore by the waves on the sands of Viareggio'. Surely this was the proper place for the statue: 'it would become an object of continual pilgrimages, and would add fame and honour to a small spot which hitherto boasts of no other glory than that of having received upon its sands the corpse of one of the greatest of English poets'.[4] By this time, however, Lady Shelley was getting ready to forgive Oxford, and had turned for advice to one of the best-connected men in the University, Benjamin Jowett, the Master of Balliol. Would Oxford welcome the monument, she asked him, and was there was a suitable site for it, *'under cover'*?

The memorials of Shelley

Lady Shelley admired Jowett; so much so that the great man's photograph by Julia Margaret Cameron was on display in one of the guest rooms at her home. At the beginning of the year she had sought his advice on another pressing matter, namely what she should do with the family archive in her keeping. Two-thirds of the archive, she had decided, would remain in the family, but the remaining third would go to an institution, perhaps the British Museum, or the Bodleian Library. Jowett assured her that they would be well looked after in either place, but confessed that as 'an Oxford man' he would naturally like to have them in the Bodleian (of which he was one of the Curators). He invited Lady Shelley to come and see him in Oxford, and meet the Vice-Chancellor and Bodley's Librarian. 'It is hard for the world to do justice to a character like Shelley's', he told her. 'They cannot separate his social theories from his personal character.' These 'social theories', most notably free love, could not be defended, Jowett wrote, 'unless we are willing to go back to barbarism', but he acknowledged that something could nevertheless be learned from 'the innocence & goodness & disinterestedness' of Shelley's character.[5]

Figure 5 Louis Antoine Philippe, duc de Montpensier, portrait of P.B. Shelley as a boy. Oxford, Bodleian Library, Shelley relics 7.

As for the monument, two places immediately occurred to Jowett: the library of University College (although the association of the college and Shelley was, he admitted 'rather unfortunate'), and the gallery of the Bodleian (the present Upper Reading Room), where 'P.B.S. would be near his books & MSS'. 'Though I do not consider Oxford an unsuitable place for a Memorial to any great literary man', he concluded, 'I have no doubt that for Shelley, Rome or Florence would be far preferable. Yet we should be glad to welcome him back to the Scenes of his youth. Our conduct to him was, in those days, what might have been expected of us, but we, of our time, would gladly be reconciled with the injured shadow'.[6] As soon as he learned the scale of the monument, and its weight (10 tons), Jowett made up his mind: 'It should be offered to University College', he wrote decisively; but, he was quick to add, 'I still think that the Bodleian is the fitter place for the papers, and not University College.'[7]

On Jowett's recommendation Lady Shelley wrote to the Master of University College, James Franck Bright, offering a 'Monument of P.B. Shelley the poet, once a member of your College', on condition that 'it be placed in a suitable position & light. The expense of fixing it will partly be incurred by myself, the remainder of the sum may, it is hoped, be raised by the poet's admirers. The place was one in which he must have passed many happy hours, and the circumstances under which he left the College are hardly worth considering now.'[8] Bright was enthusiastic, and in December 1891 was pleased to report that the Fellows wished to accept the monument, had identified a suitable site, and were ready to make the necessary alterations. In June the following year Jowett was able to tell Lady Shelley that the Curators of the Bodleian Library had accepted her offer of the Shelley papers: 'We shall be happy to take charge of the papers whenever you like to send them', he assured her. 'The Memorials of Shelley will not be uncared for in their last resting place.'[9]

Lady Shelley's gifts to University College and the Bodleian in 1892 were timed to mark the centenary of Shelley's birth. Neither would be completed, however, until the following year. 'I am looking forward to placing these treasures under your care', Lady Shelley wrote to Bodley's Librarian, E.W.B. Nicholson, on 23 April 1893; 'for more than forty years they have been more precious to me than anything I possess and I believe that by placing them now in the Bodleian Library they will become objects of interest to the world at large & well cared for when I am no longer here.'[10] On 13 June she came to Oxford and personally handed over her treasures. They included a miniature portrait of Shelley as a boy, copied by Reginald Easton after an original by the duc de Montpensier; seven of Shelley's and Mary Shelley's notebooks; a leather box containing their correspondence; a manuscript copy of Shelley's greatest prose work *A Defence of Poetry*, neatly copied out by Mary Shelley for the printer; four of Shelley's early pamphlets, including a copy of the infamous, and now highly sought after *Necessity of Atheism*; and a copy of Sophocles which, it was said, Shelley had been clutching during his final moments before drowning. At Lady Shelley's request, a number of items, including the Sophocles, were put on public display.

The following day Lady Shelley formally opened the Shelley Memorial at University College with the words quoted at the beginning of this chapter. In his speech of thanks, the Master welcomed back the poet whom, eighty-three years earlier, his predecessors had summarily expelled. Bright was a progressive figure in the University, and had done much to improve the standards of teaching there. He argued that theological degrees could be awarded to non-members of the Church of England, and supported proposals to allow women to take degrees. Oxford, he said in his speech, 'must advance with the world, must expand and be open to all new influences', and he 'could not conceive any more true emblem of the present century than the great poet whose effigy they had now received'. The Memorial was 'a sort of emblem and a symbol to them of a rubbing out of old ill-wills and old ill-feelings, and of a perfectly peaceful feeling towards that great man'. His predecessors, he said, had acted as anyone would have done at that time: 'the very greatness of the man had rendered him open to that sort of treatment'. His hatred of falseness and oppression had singled him out as a true rebel, and he had been treated as a rebel. But, Bright went on, 'the rebel of eighty years ago' was 'the hero of the present century.' Shelley was 'a prophet who prophesied good things and not bad'.

It is open to question whether the Memorial truly represents Bright's outspoken rebel and prophet, the man whose 'social principles', Jowett believed, would result in barbarism. Onslow Ford's supine figure, though beautifully designed and carved, is unworldly and epicene (it has been suggested that it was carved from a female model), while Champneys's setting encourages a quasi-religious response, not a devotion to reform and free speech. The Memorial recalls Matthew Arnold's description of Shelley as a 'beautiful and ineffectual angel, beating in the void his luminous wings in vain'[11]. It is hardly surprising that an anonymous author, reporting the opening of the Shelley Memorial in the *Speaker*, had got a little carried away:

> The college which first took up the world's case against him can now pay back some of the world's debt in giving him vindication and repose. It is as if the restless sea, in whose breast he had been tossed all those years, had laid him at last upon the threshold from which he had been first cast forth.

Figure 6 Shelley's gold watch. Attached are seals belonging to Shelley and Mary Shelley. Oxford, Bodleian Library, Shelley relics (g).

His college has taken him in. The old walls enfold him in a protecting embrace. The mellow genius of the place whispers to him soothingly. In the quadrangle outside the ancient turf is green in sun and shade. The chimes of Magdalen steal gently through the trees upon the evening air.... For Shelley's storm-driven spirit where so fitting a spot to rest as amid the benign peace of Oxford.[12]

In 1894 Lady Shelley returned to the Bodleian with a few more treasures: a miniature of Mary Shelley by Easton (a companion to the miniature of Shelley as a boy); the poet's watch and gold chain, attached to which were a number of the seals Shelley and Mary used for their letters, including an amethyst engraved 'Mary Shelley'; and a locket containing locks of Shelley's and Mary's hair, and bearing an inscription modified from Petrarch: '*Beati gli occhi che lo vider vivo*' (Blessed the eyes that saw him alive). They joined the treasures already on display, and placed Shelley in the company of his noble-minded wife. 'I went to Oxford on Thursday to place my last treasures in the Bodleian', Lady Shelley wrote to her friend Richard Garnett at the British Museum, 'they have given me a cabinet all to myself with a glass top under which are placed the relics I have treasured so dearly for the last forty years of my life – It is a great happiness to have seen them there & to know that they are considered the most valuable collection they have ever received.'[13]

For more than forty years Lady Shelley had, as she put it when opening the Shelley Memorial, 'striven to give the world a just impression' of the poet's character. She had now succeeded in casting

her image of the poet in stone in Shelley's old college, and in displaying
a suitably suggestive selection of relics in a glass case in the Bodleian.
But the papers – those she had presented to the Bodleian, and those
she would bequeath to the family – were another matter. The literary
and intellectual riches, the tragedies and emotional upheavals recorded
in ink on its thousands of pages, could not be so shaped, or confined
to a single, judicious impression. Lady Shelley had herself hinted that
secrets still lay hidden within the archive by stipulating that the box
of Shelley's and Mary's correspondence 'should until the Centenary of
Shelley's death in the year 1922 be kept apart, and not be allowed to
be seen by any person except the Curators and Bodley's Librarian, and
that no copy of any portion of them should be taken by any one'. After 8
July 1922 (the centenary of Shelley's death), 'permission to inspect these
papers may be granted by the Curators, provided that an application
is laid before them at their regular meetings and that the applicant is
known to them or some of them.'

Jowett had described the Shelley memorials as arriving at their 'final
resting-place'. But the Shelley family archive has never really been about
rest. Its story begins not with Shelley, but with William Godwin and
Mary Wollstonecraft.

2

William Godwin and Mary Wollstonecraft

The Journal

In April 1788, when he was thirty-two, William Godwin began a journal. He maintained it for the next forty-eight years, making his final entry on 26 March 1836, less than two weeks before his death at the age of eighty-one. For most of those forty-eight years Godwin followed, so far as he could, the same daily routine: before breakfast he read from one of the Greek or Latin classics; in the morning he read and wrote; in the afternoons he became sociable and sought out one or more of his many London friends, with whom he enjoyed arguing, dining, and going to the theatre. His journal reflects this orderly life. Each of the thirty-two, soft-bound notebooks is of uniform size and shape; each one has been neatly divided into days and weeks in red ink. The entries themselves (in black ink) are brief and matter-of-fact. Godwin records what he has read, what he has written, and the people he has seen. Occasionally he is cryptic: he writes in Latin or French, or employs a form of personal code. The journal is at once highly informative and profoundly reticent.[1]

Godwin's entry for Sunday, 13 November 1791 records a dinner with the radical bookseller Joseph Johnson at his premises in St Paul's Churchyard; his fellow guests included Thomas Paine and Mary Wollstonecraft: 'Dine at Johnson's with Paine, Shovet & Wolstencraft; talk of monarchy, Tooke, Johnson, Voltaire, pursuits and religion.' It should have been a stimulating conversation. In France the nobility had been abolished and the royal family imprisoned. In Birmingham, the house of the scientist Joseph Priestley, who was sympathetic to the French Revolution, had been attacked and burned. Thomas Paine had just published *The Rights of Man*, a brilliant reply to Edmund Burke's recent attack on the Revolution, *Reflections on the Revolution in France*. Wollstonecraft had published her own reply to Burke, *A Vindication of the Rights of Men*, in 1790. But Godwin later described the occasion as 'not fortunate'. He had come to hear Paine, a reserved man, but instead found himself listening to Wollstonecraft, who was not at all reserved. It was the first time he and Wollstonecraft had met, and their names meant little to each other. Godwin had begun life as a dissenting

Feby 10. Su. 20 minutes before 8. ———
————————————

————————————

Montagu, M, miss G & Fanny dine.
11 M. Carlisle calls: Montagu at tea.

12. Tu. Johnson & At n call: Montagu &
miss G at tea.

13. W. At n, Ogne n & Dyson n call: mus^r
removes: Fenwicks sup from Fordyce:
write to Inchbald, Tuthil & Parr.

14. Th. Write to mrs Cotton. Barbauld on Devotion, p. 22. Fenwicks & PV ‡ sup.

15. F. Funeral: M's lodgings. Write to Carlisle.
Pursley, p. 50. Fawcet dines; adv. Fenwicks.

16. Sa. Pursley, p. 126: Mary, p. 187, fin. Call
on McKeveley, w. Fenwick: Fawcet dines: Fanny at home: At calls.

minister, and now earned a precarious living as a literary hack, turning out reviews, novels and sermons in great profusion. Wollstonecraft had worked as a governess and a schoolteacher, and now, like Godwin, lived by her pen. Alongside her journalism and translation work she had published a novel, *Mary*, in 1788. After this first encounter, they parted 'mutually displeased with each other'.[2]

Mary Wollstonecraft's name does not appear again in Godwin's journal until 8 January 1796, when they met over tea at the home of the writer Mary Hays. By this time they were both famous: Wollstonecraft as the author of *A Vindication of the Rights of Woman*, published in 1792, Godwin as the author of *An Enquiry Concerning Political Justice*, his great argument for philosophical anarchism published in 1793, and a novel, *Things As They Are, or, the Adventures of Caleb Williams*, published the following year. Since their last meeting Wollstonecraft had suffered: she had been to revolutionary France, and there given birth to a daughter, Fanny, by an American merchant, Gilbert Imlay. On returning to London, and finding Imlay unfaithful, she had twice tried to commit suicide. This time she and Godwin slowly struck up a friendship; in August 1796 they became lovers. Godwin carefully recorded their intimacy in his journal using the phrases 'chez elle' and 'chez moi', and a system of dots and dashes.[3]

In December Mary Wollstonecraft found she was pregnant, and on 29 March 1797 she and Godwin married. Their friends were surprised, for they had both argued strongly against the institution of marriage in their writing. On 30 August, Mary gave birth to their daughter, Mary Wollstonecraft Godwin; 'Birth of Mary, 20 minutes after eleven at night' noted Godwin. Ten days later Mary Wollstonecraft died from complications following the birth. Godwin wrote, simply, '20 minutes before 8', and a series of lines.

Thus did Godwin record in the pages of his journal, in an abbreviated and touching fashion, his brief life with Mary Wollstonecraft.

The letters

Throughout their time together Godwin and Wollstonecraft preferred to live independently, and communicated, to an unusual extent, by correspondence. They sent each other letters on a daily basis, addressed to 'Mr Godwin' and 'Mrs Imlay' (later 'Mrs Godwin'), which they either sent by messenger or, occasionally, delivered in person. Together they provide an eloquent expression of their relationship, its sympathies and disagreements, assertions and vulnerabilities, intimacies and misunderstandings. On the morning of 17 August 1796, for example, Mary wrote to Godwin:

Figure 8 Page from William Godwin's journal [with dates digitally enhanced]. On 10 September 1797 he records the time of Mary Wollstonecraft's death. Oxford, Bodleian Library, MS. Abinger e. 8, fol. 26v.

I have not lately passed so painful a night as the last. I feel that I cannot speak clearly on the subject to you; let me then briefly explain myself now I am alone. Yet, struggling as I have been a long time to attain peace of mind (or apathy) I am afraid to trace emotions to their source, which border on agony.

Is it not sufficient to tell you that I am thoroughly out of humour with myself? Mortified and humbled, I scarcely know why – still, despising false delicacy I almost fear that I have lost sight of the true. Could a wish have transported me to France or Italy, last night, I should have caught up my Fanny and been off in a twinkle, though convinced that it is my mind, not the place, which requires changing. My imagination is for ever betraying me into fresh misery, and I perceive that I shall be a child to the end of the chapter. You talk of roses which grow profusely in every path of life – I catch at them; but only encounter the thorns. –

I would not be unjust for the world – I can only say that you appear to me to have acted injudiciously; and that full of your own feelings, little as I comprehend them, you forgot mine – or do not understand my character. It is my turn to have a fever to day – I am not well – I am hurt – But I mean not to hurt you. Consider what has passed as a fever of your imagination; one of the slight mortal shakes to which you are liable – and I – will become again a *Solitary Walker*. Adieu! I was going to add God bless you! –

At one o'clock Godwin composed a reply:

You do not know how honest I am. I swear to you that I told you nothing but the strict & literal truth, when I described to you the manner in which you set my imagination on fire on Saturday. For six & thirty hours I could think of nothing else. I longed inexpressibly to have you in my arms. Why did not I come to you? I am a fool.... I know the acuteness of your feelings, and there is perhaps nothing upon earth that would give me so pungent a remorse, as to add to your unhappiness. Do not hate me. Indeed I do not deserve it. Do not cast me off. Do not again become a *solitary walker*.... Send me word that I may call on you in a day or two. Do you not see, while I exhort you to be a philosopher, how painfully acute are my own feelings? I need some soothing, though I cannot ask it from you.

'I like your last – may I call it *love* letter – better than the first', replied Mary at two o'clock,

and can I give you higher proof of my esteem than to tell you, the style of my letter will whether I will or no, that it has calmed my mind – a mind that had been painfully active all the morning, haunted by old sorrows that seemed to come forward with new force to sharpen the present anguish – Well! Well – it is almost gone – I mean all unreasonable fears – and a whole train of tormenters, which you have routed – I can scarcely describe to you their ugly shapes so quickly do they vanish – and let them go, we will not bring them back by talking of them. You may see me when you please.[4]

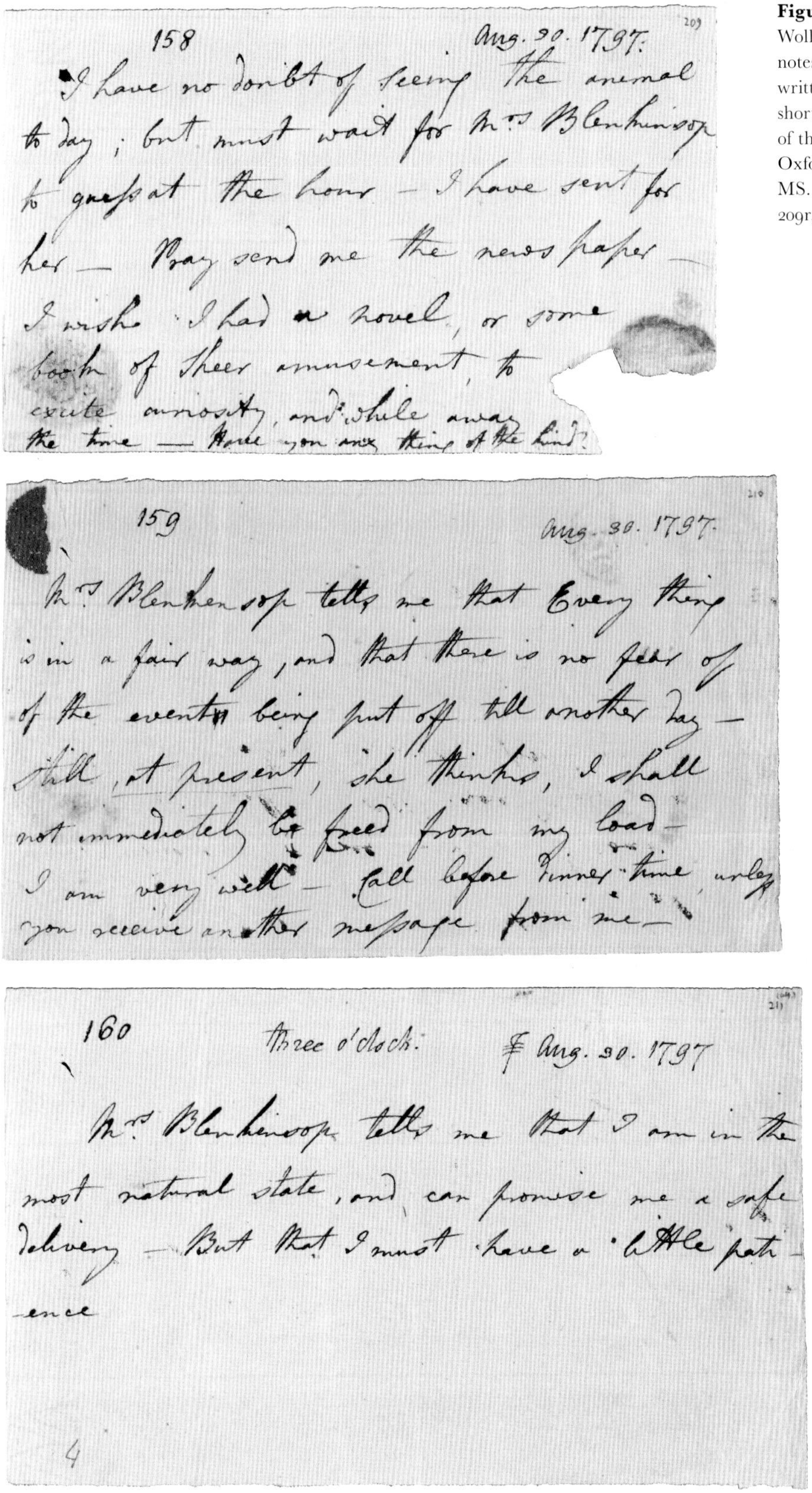

158   *Aug. 30. 1797.*

I have no doubt of seeing the animal to day; but must wait for Mrs Blenkinsop to guess at the hour — I have sent for her — Pray send me the news paper — I wish I had a novel, or some book of sheer amusement, to excite curiosity, and while away the time — Have you any thing of the kind?

159   *Aug. 30. 1797.*

Mrs Blenkensop tells me that Every thing is in a fair way, and that there is no fear of of the event being put off till another day — Still, at present, she thinks, I shall not immediately be freed from my load — I am very well — Call before dinner time, unless you receive another message from me —

160   *Three o'clock.*   *Aug. 30. 1797*

Mrs Blenkinsop tells me that I am in the most natural state, and can promise me a safe delivery — But that I must have a little patience

4

Figure 9 Mary Wollstonecraft's last three notes to William Godwin, written on 30 August 1797, shortly before the birth of their daughter Mary. Oxford, Bodleian Library, MS. Abinger c. 40, fols 209r, 210r, 211r.

Long, carefully composed letters such as these are mixed with shorter notes, many of them dashed off on scraps of paper torn hurriedly from larger sheets, then folded into thin strips, addressed and sealed. Often they provide brief updates on the writer's state of mind and health; at other times they are prompted by everyday matters like appointments, the need for wine, more ink, or certain books. Three notes, written by Wollstonecraft to Godwin shortly before giving birth to their daughter, movingly conclude their correspondence. Godwin has added the date, 30 August 1797, to each of these notes, and on the final one has also written the time, 'three o'clock'.

Posthumous works and memoirs

In the weeks following Mary Wollstonecraft's death Godwin gathered together her papers. He had decided to produce an edition of her un-published works. There was the manuscript of the novel she was writing at her death, *The Wrongs of Woman, or, Maria*, a few fragments such as part of 'The Cave of Fancy, A Tale', and parts of 'Letters on the Management of Infants' and 'Lessons for Children'. There were also the letters, over a hundred in number, which Mary had written to Gilbert Imlay and which Imlay, at her request, had agreed to return. They were deeply personal expressions of love and, increasingly, anguish, but Godwin, who prized objectivity, detached them from their origins and looked at them from a purely literary point of view. He judged them equal, if not superior, to Goethe's great account of unrequited love, *The Sorrows of Young Werther*, an epistolary novel first published in English in 1779.

Godwin was also determined to write an account of Mary Wollstonecraft's life. Here he had notes taken from his long, searching conversations with her about her past. He also wrote to her family and friends asking for information. Joseph Johnson supplied him with details about her early life, and gave him the numerous letters he had received from her. Others, however, were less forthcoming. The painter Henry Fuseli, who had once been the object of Mary's fervent affections, had kept her letters to him, but refused to share them. It is said that he allowed Godwin a quick glimpse of the letters in a drawer, then slammed the drawer shut. Mary Wollstonecraft's sister Everina thought Godwin was acting hastily, and told him so:

> When Eliza and I first learnt your intention of publishing immediately my sister Mary's life, we concluded, that you only meant a sketch to prevent your design concerning her memoirs from being anticipated. We thought your application to us rather premature … At a future day we would willingly have given whatever information was necessary; and even now we would not have shrunk from the task however anxious we may be to avoid reviving

the recollections it would raise, or loath to fall into the pain of thoughts it must lead to, did we suppose it possible to accomplish the work you have undertaken in the time you specify. The questions you have addressed to me confirm this opinion; and I am sorry to perceive you are inclined to be minute, when I think it is impossible for you to be tolerably accurate.[5]

Such was Godwin's industry and assiduity, however, that he succeeded in publishing, at the beginning of 1798, *Posthumous Works of the Author of a Vindication of the Rights of Woman* (in four volumes) and *A Memoir of the Author of a Vindication of the Rights of Woman*. The *Posthumous Works* included most of Wollstonecraft's literary fragments, and her letters to Joseph Johnson. A good quarter of it was taken up by her letters to Imlay. In publishing these letters so soon after the writer's death, albeit in a slightly edited form, Godwin was showing unprecedented candour, but as far as he was concerned their outstanding literary merit outweighed mere personal qualms: 'The following Letters may possibly be found to contain the finest examples of sentiment and passion ever presented to the world.… They are the offspring of a glowing imagination, and a heart penetrated with the passion it essays to describe.'[6] He even provided a few explanatory footnotes.

The *Memoir* was, if anything, even more candid. Godwin approached it in the belief that the story of Mary Wollstonecraft's life would be an inspiration to others, that it could only benefit by being told with complete frankness and truth, and that it was his duty, as someone who knew her intimately, to tell that story. He wrote in a preface:

> It seldom happens that such a person passes through life, without being the subject of thoughtless calumny, or malignant representation. It cannot happen that the public at large should be on a footing with their intimate acquaintance, and be the observer of those virtues which discover themselves principally in personal intercourse. Every benefactor of mankind is more or less influenced by a liberal passion for fame; and survivors only pay a debt due to these benefactors, when they assert and establish on their part, the honour they loved. The justice which is thus done to the illustrious dead, converts into the fairest source of animation and encouragement to those who would follow them in the same career.[7]

So the reader learns of the abuse Mary suffered at the hands of her brutal, drunken father; of her ardent but depressive temperament; of 'the friendship that subsisted between Mary and Mr Fuseli'; of 'that species of connection for which her heart secretly panted' with 'Mr Gilbert Imlay, native of the United States of North America' and their illegitimate daughter; and of her two suicide attempts. Arriving at what he calls 'to the last branch of her history, the connection between Mary and myself', Godwin remarks:

this I shall relate with the same simplicity that has pervaded every other part of my narrative. If there ever were any motives of prudence or delicacy, that could impose a qualification upon the story, they are now over. They could have no relation but to factitious rules of decorum. There are no circumstances of her life, that, in the judgment of honour and reason, could brand her with disgrace. Never did there exist a human being, that needed, with less fear, expose all their actions, and call upon the universe to judge them.[8]

He proceeds to give a detailed and unflinching account of Mary's final illness, and of her lack of conventional Christian faith. These concluding chapters are rendered more powerful and moving by Godwin's personal involvement, and his open appreciation of Mary's benign influence on his character: 'This light was lent to me for a very short period, and is now extinguished for ever!'

The literary world strongly objected to Godwin's publication of Mary Wollstonecraft's letters to Imlay, and deplored the *Memoir*. Robert Southey declared that Godwin had shown 'a want of all feeling in stripping his dead wife naked'. The reviewers saw Mary's personal behaviour and unorthodox beliefs not as exemplary, as evidence of a remarkable independence of thought and sensibility, but as proof of moral depravity. 'This appears to us to be a very extraordinary method of doing honour to her memory', commented the *New Annual Register*. 'And we should be sorry, could we suppose the moral taste of the world to be so vitiated as that these Memoirs would be much read, without exciting lively emotions of disgust and concern.'[9] Such a reaction is to be expected at a time when biographical exposure, so commonplace today, was unknown, but a more sympathetic response came to Godwin in the form of a sincere and confused letter, misspelled and badly punctuated, sent to him from Warrington. He kept the letter.

Having read a Book intitled the Life of Mary Woolstonecraft Godwin being compiled by her Husband, I perused it with avidity, the beging I exceedingly gratified with, but felt hurt when I arrived at the place where all Woes commenced. A Woman of her exalted mind forgets herself every tongue is ready to condemn who can be Silent, not her own Sex I am sure she who shou'd have steped forward in asserting the rights of Woman, to so soon swerve from the Paths of Rectitude is unfortunate to the last degree. She shou'd have presented us with an Example worthy of Immitation. She could teach better a good deal than she did Practice Her Intelectual strength was superior to most either Male or Female. Who can possibly vindicate this Conduct, not a Woman. I do so regret MW's faults that I express my self with difficulty. Modesty which she speaks of so divinely – is poorly supported. What must I or any one else suppose from these glaring of all defects and exposed by a Person so nearly and intimately Connected as you have been –

I commiserate her sufferings, and shou'd not have revived them in your rememberance, had I not heard this production so severely censured –

I am a true friend to my own Sex & sympathize with such of them, who act with impropriety – But do hope you will never make her Children – acquainted with their dear Mother's misfortunes – set all her amiable Qualities before them. They are worthy of their immitation Her Sorrows were more than often fall to the lost of the generality of females I seem particularly interested for the Infant she had when surrounded by distress in a strange Land – the affection you bore this dear lamented Woman will tend to produce a tenderness to the orphan Daughter.

With best wishes for your Wlfare I am your sincere friend tho' unknown A Lancashire Woman RW —[10]

Remains

Godwin believed that literary remains, including letters, should be published, and that it was the duty of survivors to defend writers from the ill-informed accusations of their contemporaries, and honour their 'liberal passion for fame' by honestly telling their story for posterity. He also believed that the key to their characters and opinions lay in the scenes and incidents of their lives. Motivated by his own passion for fame, he therefore carefully preserved his own papers for the benefit of those who survived him. But he appears to have thought that, once published (or rejected as unpublishable), a manuscript's job was done. He kept the precious letters and notes Mary Wollstonecraft had sent him, arranging them chronologically with his letters to her, and numbering the combined sequence from 1 to 160; but otherwise he seems to have thrown her manuscripts away. The original letters she wrote to Joseph Johnson and Gilbert Imlay have not survived, and it is likely that Godwin disposed of them. The manuscripts of the literary works he published posthumously are no longer in the archive, and one work, a comic drama, he neither published nor preserved: '[It] appeared to me to be in so crude and imperfect a state', he wrote in the *Memoir*, 'that I judged it most respectful to her memory to commit it to the flames.'

So the Wollstonecraft manuscripts which Godwin ultimately left to their daughter Mary were rather few in number. Mary grew up, nevertheless, with her mother's image constantly before her. She read the books, including Godwin's *Memoir*, and talked to her mother's friends; the portrait, painted by John Opie in the last year of her mother's life, hung above the fireplace in Godwin's study. Lady Shelley later told a friend how Mary 'read a great deal, and when worries and troubles grew too many to bear, she would go and sit by her mother's grave in St Pancras and there spend long hours with her precious books'. Later, she and her lover, Percy Bysshe Shelley, would meet at the grave and, said Lady Shelley, 'have long talks'.[11]

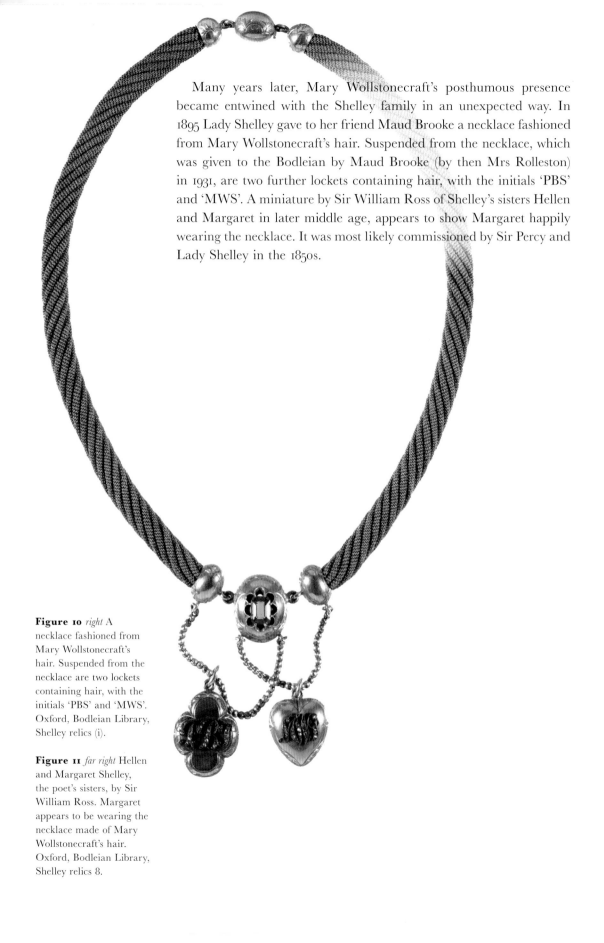

Many years later, Mary Wollstonecraft's posthumous presence became entwined with the Shelley family in an unexpected way. In 1895 Lady Shelley gave to her friend Maud Brooke a necklace fashioned from Mary Wollstonecraft's hair. Suspended from the necklace, which was given to the Bodleian by Maud Brooke (by then Mrs Rolleston) in 1931, are two further lockets containing hair, with the initials 'PBS' and 'MWS'. A miniature by Sir William Ross of Shelley's sisters Hellen and Margaret in later middle age, appears to show Margaret happily wearing the necklace. It was most likely commissioned by Sir Percy and Lady Shelley in the 1850s.

Figure 10 *right* A necklace fashioned from Mary Wollstonecraft's hair. Suspended from the necklace are two lockets containing hair, with the initials 'PBS' and 'MWS'. Oxford, Bodleian Library, Shelley relics (i).

Figure 11 *far right* Hellen and Margaret Shelley, the poet's sisters, by Sir William Ross. Margaret appears to be wearing the necklace made of Mary Wollstonecraft's hair. Oxford, Bodleian Library, Shelley relics 8.

✥ 3 ✥

Godwin and the Shelleys

The philosopher

William Godwin's correspondence with Mary Wollstonecraft survived in his archive along with over 1,800 other letters. He saved and organised these letters like an archivist. His outgoing correspondence is preserved in the form of his original drafts and in the neat file copies made by himself or members of his household. For ten years (1795–1805) he even employed an early portable copying machine, of a type patented by James Watt & Co. in 1780 and also used by Benjamin Franklin, Thomas Jefferson and Joseph Priestley. Some seventy-five complete letters, and a few fragmentary ones, have survived in this form, identifiable by the flimsy, translucent paper and special ink required for the process.[1]

Godwin successfully combined long periods of solitary study with sociability. He kept an open house, and was a frequent, and argumentative, guest at the homes of his many friends and acquaintances. This, he believed, was how a philosopher should live. The writers, publishers, scientists, politicians and actors with whom he corresponded include Samuel Taylor Coleridge, Charles Lamb, William Wordsworth, Elizabeth Inchbald, Richard Brinsley Sheridan, William Hazlitt, Thomas Malthus, Thomas Lawrence, Robert Peel, John Philip Kemble and Humphry Davy. 'To Willm Godwin, Philosopher' Mary Wollstonecraft addressed one of her letters to him, no doubt with tongue in cheek, but others addressed him in this way with complete seriousness. 'Why, my dear Philosopher, why will you continue to think me unworthily capricious?' the actress Mary Robinson wrote to him in the last year of her life. 'I really wish to cultivate your esteem, to deserve your approbation. … I had, before I ever saw you, formed an Idea, – that you were fastidious, stern, austere, and abstracted from worldly enjoyments. I was to contemplate the Philosopher, the enlightened, studious observer of mankind'.[2]

On 25 November 1800 a militia sergeant named Martin Smart wrote to Godwin as 'an utter stranger' in order to point out 'some of the literal and grammatical inaccuracies which I have noticed in a frequent and

Figure 12 Portrait of William Godwin by James Northcote (1802). Bequeathed to the National Portrait Gallery by Lady Shelley. © National Portrait Gallery, London.

attentive perusal of that work, and which you may probably wish to correct'. He proceeded to fill the next two and half sides of paper with his minute observations:

> My next remark is on the different constructions of the same verbs in the course of your work. Thus I find 'originate' used actively in volume 2. page 63. line 6. from bottom; passively in the same volume, page 280. line 12. and page 442. line 2. from bottom; neutrally, which is surely its most usual acceptation, in volume 1. page 57. note, line 6. page 194. line 17. volume 2. page 67. line last, page 105. line 2. from bottom: 'convert' is…

and so it goes on.[3] Not all writers would welcome such relentless pedantry; Godwin was delighted.

Five days after Smart, the American politician William Green Munford wrote to Godwin from New York with a request:

> An election for President takes place the week after next – The republicans will support & probably carry Mr Jefferson & Mr Burr. A gentleman in this city, a warm admirer of the life & writing of Mrs Godwin would be extremely obliged to you to permit a polygraphic copy of her portrait which hangs in one of your rooms, to be made & forwarded to me with the books – It is intended to hold the most distinguished place among his most precious reliques – It is placed at the head of the catalogue, & should be first attended to.[4]

Then, the following week a woman signing herself 'R.M.' wrote Godwin urgently from Liverpool:

> Are your *ideas* really equal to your *theory* or do you write for *others* and *think* for *yourself*? perhaps you may imagine me mad, and be surprised nay angry, at this address from a *stranger* – well you shall never be troubled with her again *if so* —
>
> Hitherto I have never suffered my actions to be shackled by the tyranny of *custom* – the consequence is, I have but *one* friend, *few* acquaintances and *no* lover men in general confer tameness in a woman (which they dignify, or rather *burlesque* with the name of sensibility) to the noble sentiment of *independence* – you – *you* are different – therefore naturally enthusiastic and warm where I *admire* I cannot debar myself the pleasure of telling you so. – I heard you spoken of in a certain company as too free in disseminating your opinions – I felt my heart bound, and the moment I went home, sent for all I could collect of your writings – now dissolved in tears of extasy – now *lost* in admiration, now elevated with *enthusiasm* – now transported with the *intensity* of my feelings, I read and, and paused and read again – I languished to *converse* with the immortal author – to gaze at him *unseen* – but to identify him in the passing crowd … I am lost buried, in more than cimmerian darkness, – take pity on me then – *write* – *let* me be edified[5]

In the 1800s Godwin's status as a philosopher declined, and letters
like these became less frequent. After Mary Wollstonecraft's death he
became a family man, and his correspondence is increasingly about
money. He raised their daughter Mary, and adopted Wollstonecraft's
first daughter Fanny Imlay (who thus became Fanny Godwin). In 1801
he married a widow, Mary Jane Clairmont, who already had two young
children, Charles and Clara Mary Jane (who would later call herself
Claire). In 1803 the second Mrs Godwin gave birth to a son, William
Godwin Junior. In 1805, in an attempt to support this unorthodox
family (none of the five children shared the same parents), Godwin
established a bookselling and publishing business in his wife's name. It
was time consuming, but unprofitable, and Godwin spent a good deal
of time requesting financial assistance from anyone he could think of,
from trusted patrons such as the Wedgwoods to people he barely knew.
Here he could show considerable ingenuity; John Lens, for instance,
must have been rather surprised to receive the following letter:

> Sir, – It is a thousand to one whether your recollect a little boy to whom you
> did a kind action between 50 and 60 years ago, and who has never seen you
> since. You, I daresay, have done so many kind actions since, that this may
> well be obliterated from your mind.
>
> We met at Mr Christian's dancing-school at Norwich. You were almost
> a man grown, and I was perhaps about twelve years of age. You and your
> sister and a Miss Carter were, I believe, at the head of the school. Miss
> Carter was a very plain girl, but a good dancer. I was in reality no dancer at
> all. It so happened that one day in your hearing I said, thinking perhaps of
> nothing, I should like for once to dance with Miss Carter. You immediately
> answered, I will take care that you shall, and accordingly you brought it
> about. This is altogether a trifle, but it has a hundred times recurred to my
> memory.
>
> We have since run a different career. I have written 'Caleb Williams' and
> 'St Leon,' and a number of other books. Did you ever hear of those books?
> And if you did, did your quondam school-fellow at the dancing-school
> ever occur to your mind? You have been perhaps more usefully employed
> in an honourable profession. The consequence is, you are rich, and I am
> – something else.

He then gives Lens a brief account of his unfortunate financial history,
and his current, desperate position: 'the beginning of November must
decide my good or ill fortune.… It is by a very slender, and almost
invisible thread that I can hope to have any hold upon you, but I am
resolved not to desert myself'.[6]

No reply from Lens survives among Godwin's papers. One
correspondent, however, writing to Godwin in January 1812, was clearly
an avid reader of his books: 'The name of Godwin has been used to excite
in me feelings of reverence and admiration, I have been accustomed to

Figure 13 Portrait of
Percy Shelley by Amelia
Curran (1819). Bequeathed
to the National Portrait
Gallery by Lady Shelley.
© National Portrait
Gallery, London.

consider him a luminary too dazzling for the darkness which surrounds
him.' The writer goes on to say, not altogether flatteringly (and, in fact,
falsely), that he had assumed Godwin had died: 'Considering then these
feelings you will not be surprised at the inconceivable emotions with
which I learned your existence and your dwelling. I had enrolled your
name on the list of the honorable dead. I had felt regret that the glory
of your being had passed from this earth of ours.'[7] Godwin wrote back
immediately. 'Write to Shelley' he noted in his journal.

Public notoriety

Although he never quite matched the level of notoriety achieved by his
friend Lord Byron, Percy Bysshe Shelley had an unusually eventful life.
A few months after his expulsion from Oxford in 1811 he eloped with the
sixteen-year-old Harriet Westbrook; they were married in Edinburgh in
August. Alienated from his family, he spent the next two years wandering
restlessly around Britain: from Scotland to the Lakes, then to Ireland,
Wales, Devon, and back to Wales. His radical political activities in
each of these places brought him to the attention of the authorities.
A daughter, Eliza Ianthe, was born in June 1813. The following year
Shelley eloped with Godwin's sixteen-year-old daughter Mary; they, and
Claire Clairmont, spent six weeks travelling around the Continent. In
November 1814 his first son, Charles, was born to Harriet. In January
1816 his second son, William, was born to Mary. That summer Shelley,
Mary and Claire visited Lord Byron in Switzerland; Claire had already
become pregnant by Byron, and later gave birth to a daughter, Allegra.
In October 1816 Fanny Imlay, after leaving final letters for Godwin
and Shelley, committed suicide. The following month Harriet Shelley
committed suicide, and Shelley and Mary married. In 1817 the Lord
Chancellor denied Shelley custody of his two children by Harriet. Shelley
and Mary then spent four years in Italy, moving continually, and losing
their infant daughter Clara, and son William. Only one of their children
survived into adulthood: Percy Florence, born in 1819.

Some of these events were public knowledge during Shelley's
lifetime, and unsympathetic reviewers of his poems liked to refer to
them, particularly when those poems portrayed the reforming power of
human love. In a review of *The Revolt of Islam* in the *Quarterly*, published
in September 1819, John Taylor Coleridge made a knowing reference to
Shelley's Oxford career – 'a short one, and, if we mistake not, rather
abruptly terminated' – and dismissed him as 'really too young, too
ignorant, too inexperienced, and too vicious to undertake the task of
reforming any world, but the little world within his own breast'. He
ended the review with dark hints about Shelley's private behaviour:

'if we might withdraw the veil of private life, and tell what we *now* know about him, it would indeed be a disgusting picture that we should exhibit, but it would be an unanswerable comment on our text; it is not easy for those who *read only*, to conceive how much low pride, how much cold selfishness, how much unmanly cruelty are consistent with the laws of this 'universal' and 'lawless love'.[8]

'Failing in the attempt to refute Mr Shelley's philosophy, the Reviewers attack his private life', countered Shelley's close friend Leigh Hunt in the *Examiner*. 'What is the argument of this? Or what right have they to know any thing of the private life of an author? Or how would they like to have the same argument used against themselves?'[9] Shelley thought the author of the review was Robert Southey, whom he had known briefly while living in the Lake District. Southey denied it, but expressed his disapproval of Shelley's 'opinions': 'Opinions are to be judged by their effects – and what has been the fruit of yours? ... have they not brought immediate misery upon others, and guilt, which is all but irremediable, on yourself?'[10] To which Shelley replied:

> You select a single passage out of a life otherwise not only spotless but spent in impassioned pursuit of virtue, which looks like a blot, merely because I regulated my domestic arrangements without deferring to the notions of the vulgar, although I might have done so quite as conveniently had I descended to their base thoughts – this you call *guilt*. ... I am innocent of all ill, either done or intended; the consequences you allude to flowed in no respect from me. If you were my friend, I could tell you a history that would open your eyes; but I shall certainly never make the public my familiar confidant.[11]

Southey was unimpressed. He wrote back: 'At length you forsook your wife, because you were tired of her, and had found another woman more suited to your taste. You could tell me a history, you say, which would make me open my eyes. Perhaps they are already open. It is a matter of public notoriety that your wife destroyed herself.'[12]

Remaining hidden from the public gaze, for the moment at least, were the letters that passed between Shelley, Mary Shelley and William Godwin, letters written, for the most part, at times of heightened emotion and stress. It was here that much of Shelley's eye-opening history was recorded.

Private trials

Godwin and Percy Bysshe Shelley corresponded regularly for some nine months before they finally met in October 1812. Shelley's first letters to the philosopher are idealistic, rather breathless, and manage to be both self-righteous and deferential. He informed Godwin of his age

('now *nineteen*') and his situation in life ('the Son of a man of fortune in Sussex'); that he had been expelled from Oxford; that he was an atheist and a devotee of *Political Justice*; that he was 'married to a woman whose views are similar to my own'.[13] Godwin's replies followed Shelley on his hectic journeys around the country, urging caution and further thought:

> My good friend, I have read all your letters (the first perhaps excepted) with peculiar interest, and I wish it to be understood by you, unequivocally, that, as far as I can yet penetrate into your character, I conceive it to exhibit an extraordinary assemblage of lovely qualities, not without considerable defects. The defects do, and always have, arisen chiefly from this source, that you are still very young, and that in certain essential respects you do not sufficiently perceive that you are so.[14]

'Your letter affords me much food for thought', replied Shelley from Dublin; 'guide thou and direct me. – In all the weakness of my inconsistencies bear with me … I know that I am vain, that I assume a character which is perhaps unadapted to the limitedness of my experience.'[15] But Godwin was so alarmed by Shelley's activities in Ireland (his speech-making, his pamphleteering) that he immediately wrote again:

> I take up the pen again immediately on the receipt of yours, because I am desirous of making one more effort to save yourself and the Irish people from the calamities with which I see your mode of proceeding to be fraught. … Shelley, you are preparing a scene of blood. If your associations take effect to any extensive degree, tremendous consequences will follow, and hundreds by their calamities and premature fate will expiate your error. And then what will it avail you to say, I warned them against this; when I put the seed into the ground, I laid my solemn injunctions upon it that it should not germinate?[16]

A chastened Shelley replied that he had withdrawn his two inflammatory pamphlets (*Address to the Irish People* and *Proposals for an Association of Philanthropists*) and was preparing to leave Dublin.

Despite the real dangers to which Shelley was exposing himself and his family, his correspondence with Godwin has a curiously abstract quality, in which intellectual argument is conducted away from what Shelley dismissed as 'the heartless bustle of ordinary life' and its 'uninteresting details'. *Political Justice* is passed to and fro like a ghost from the past. As Godwin put it: 'Our acquaintance is a whimsical & to a certain degree anomalous one. I have never seen your face. … And till I have seen a man's face, I may say in good sooth I do not know him. Would that this whimsical & anomalous state of our acquaintance were brought to a conclusion!'[17]

It was brought to a conclusion, but not in the manner Godwin envisaged. When Shelley and Mary eloped in July 1814, correspondence of any kind between Shelley and Godwin abruptly ceased, and friendly communication would not be resumed until Shelley and Mary were married in December 1816. (Godwin noted the eloping couple's early morning departure, and Mrs Godwin's hurried pursuit in his journal: '*Five in the morning … M[ary] J[ane] for Dover*'; the marriage, at St. Mildred's Church, he recorded thus: 'Call on Mildred w. P.B.S., M.W.G., and M.J'.)

While on the Continent, and then later in London, Shelley did write several letters to Harriet. The substance of these letters, which were apparently used as evidence by Harriet's family in the ensuing court battle for custody of the children, remained unknown until copies were found by an enterprising scholar, Leslie Hotson, in the Public Record Office in the 1920s. Hotson dramatically recalled his discovery: 'A bundle was brought out, covered thick with black dust. To all appearances, the dossier had not been opened since it was tied in red tape more than a hundred years ago. At the bottom of a heap of affidavits and other original papers in the Shelley case, I came upon the quarry.'[18] A copy of one letter, however, survived in the family archive. On 19 August 1814 Godwin called on Harriet and apparently compared notes with her, for among Godwin's papers is a copy made by a member of his household (with Godwin's corrections) of a letter Shelley wrote to Harriet from Troyes:

> I write to you from this detestable Town. I write to shew you that I do not forget you. I write to urge you to come to Switzerland, where you will at least find one firm & constant friend, to whom your interests will be always dear, by whom your feelings will never wilfully be injured. From none can you expect this but me. … You shall know our adventures more detailed, if I do not hear at Neufchatel, that I am soon to have the pleasure of communicating to you in person, & of welcoming you to some sweet retreat I will procure for you among the mountains.[19]

Lady Shelley obviously valued this remarkable letter. She later separated it from Godwin's correspondence and gave it a folder all to itself.

On his return to London Shelley was faced with severe financial difficulties, and to escape his creditors he was forced to go into hiding. He and Mary only saw each other on Sundays, when arrests for bankruptcy could not be made. A number of letters they wrote during this period have survived. The first, written by Mary on 24 October 1814, is her earliest known letter to anyone:

For what a minute did I see you yesterday – is this the way my beloved that we are to live till the sixth in the morning I look for you and when I awake I turn to look on you – dearest Shelley you are solitary and uncomfortable why cannot I be with you to cheer you and to press you to my heart oh my love you have no friends why then should you be torn from the only one who has affection for you – But I shall see you tonight and that is the hope that I shall live on through the day – be happy dear Shelley and think of me – why do I say this dearest & only one I know how tenderly you love me and how you repine at this absence from me – when shall we be free from fear of treachery? – [20]

Shelley presently wrote to Mary:

I shall see you tonight. My beloved Mary fear not. Have confidence in the fortunate issue of our distresses. I am desolate & wretched in your absence. I feel disturbed & wild even to conceive that we should be separated. But this is most necessary nor must we omit caution even in our infrequent meetings. Recollect that I am lost if the People can have watched you to me. I wander restlessly about I cannot read – or even write. But this will soon pass. I should not infect my own Mary with my dejection. She has sufficient cause for disturbance to need consolation from me. Well we shall meet today. I cannot write. But I love you with so unalterable a love that the contemplation of me will serve as a letter.[21]

The silence between Godwin and Shelley during this period was broken only by Godwin's requests for money (which Shelley probably threw away when he had read them), and Shelley's cold and formal replies dating from early 1816 (which, tellingly, were separated from the family papers and found their way mostly to American libraries). It took the tragedies of Fanny Imlay's and Harriet Shelley's suicides to prompt Shelley and Godwin to renew friendly communication.

Among the family papers are four letters by Fanny Imlay (now rechristened Fanny Godwin): one to her aunt, Everina Wollstonecraft, one to Shelley and Mary, and two to Mary alone. Lady Shelley kept them in a special wrapper marked 'Fanny Godwin's Letters 1816'. The letter to Shelley and Mary is appended to a note Godwin wrote to Shelley in Switzerland in May, inevitably about money. Here Fanny reveals her vulnerability and torn loyalties: to the memory of her mother; to her stepfather; and, despite the attempts of Mrs Godwin ('Mamma') to alienate them, to Shelley and Mary:

My feeling's [sic] and tone of mind have undergone a considerable revolution for the better since I last wrote to you. I have unexpectedly seen Mr Blood brother of Fanny Blood, my mother's friend – Every thing he had told me of my mother has encreased my love and admiration of her memory … this has in some degree roused me from my torpor – I have determined never to live to be a disgrace to *such a mother* … Mary gave a great deal of pain the day I parted from you; believe my dear friend's [*sic*] that my attattchment to you has grown out of your individual worth, and talents, & perhaps also because I found the world deserted you I loved you the more. What ever faults I may have I am not *sordid* or vulgar. I love you for *your selves alone* I endeavour to be as frank to you as possible that you may understand my real character I understand from Mamma that I am your laughing stock – and the constant beacon of your ~~Ridicule~~ satire … I wish papa had not begun this letter it is so *cold* when I can assure you he speaks of you with great kindness & interest. I hope the day will not be long ere you are reconciled – [22]

In her first letter to Mary, written in July, Fanny gives her sister a description of political events in England (dutifully including Godwin's comments upon them), and asks her about Byron: 'Do answer me these questions! for w[h]ere I love the poet I should like to respect the man.' She told Mary of her belief in the divine good Shelley will do the world as a poet ('laugh at me but do not be angry with me for taking up your time with my nonsense') and the desperate state of her father's affairs. She concludes: 'I am not well my mind always keeps my body in a fever. but never mind me–'.[23] In her second letter to Mary, written on 3 October, she defends both Mrs Godwin ('Mamma and I are not great friend's [*sic*] – but alway's alive to her virtues – I am anxious to defend her from a charge so foreign to her character') and Godwin ('you know that it is of the utmost consequence for *his own* and the *world's* sake that he should *finish his novel* and is it not your and Shelley's duty to consider these things?') Mary noted in her journal the next day, '[S]tupid letter from F.'[24]

A few days later Fanny wrote notes to Godwin and Shelley from Bristol. According to Claire Clairmont, when Shelley read his note he crumpled it up and put it in his pocket, thrust his hand into his hair, and exclaimed 'I must be off.' That night Fanny took her own life in Swansea. On 13 October Godwin wrote to Shelley. His great fear, he said, was publicity:

I did indeed expect it.

I cannot but thank you for your strong expressions of sympathy. I do not see however that that sympathy can be of any service to me: but it is best.

My advice, & earnest prayer is, that you would avoid any thing that leads to publicity. Go not to Swansea. Disturb not the silent dead. Do nothing to destroy the security she so much desired, that now rests upon the event. It was, as I said, her last wish. It was the motive that led her from London to Bristol, & from Bristol to Swansea.

I said that your sympathy could be of no service to me. But I retract the assertion. By observing what I have just recommended to you, it may be of infinite service. Think what is the situation of my wife & myself, now deprived of all our children but the youngest; & do not expose us to those idle questions, which to a mind in anguish is one of the severest of all trials.

We are at this moment in doubt whether during the first shock we shall not say that she is gone to Ireland to her aunt, a thing that had been in contemplation. Do not take from us the power to exercise our own discretion. You shall hear again tomorrow.

What I have most of all in horror is the public papers; & I thank you for caution as it might act on this.

We have so conducted ourselves that not one person in our house has the smallest apprehension of the truth. Our feelings are less tumultuous than deep: God only knows what they may become.

The following is one expression in the letter to us, written from Bristol on Tuesday. 'I depart immediately to the spot from which I hope never to be removed.'[25]

Like Shelley, Godwin does not appear to have kept his last letter from Fanny, so this short quotation is all we have. The manuscript of Fanny's final note, written to no one in particular and published in the Swansea *Cambrian* on 12 October 1816, has likewise disappeared. The letter that Harriet Shelley composed shortly before her suicide has, however, survived, but not in the family archive. Written in December 1816 to her sister, her parents and Shelley, it is now in the Carl H. Pforzheimer Collection in New York. Only one letter in the family archive relates in any detailed way to Harriet's last days. Written by Shelley to Mary during the subsequent custody battle for the children, rather than the immediate aftermath of his wife's death, it offers a heated and rather garbled version of events:

This process is the most insidiously malignant that can be conceived. They have filed a bill, to say that I published Queen Mab, that I avow myself to be an atheist & a republican; with some other imputations of an infamous nature. This by Chancery law I must *deny* or *admit* upon oath, & then it seems that it rests in the grounds for refusing me my children. ...

They do not tell Harriet's story: I mean the circumstances of her death, in these allegations against me. – They evidently feel that it make[s] against themselves. They attack you & Godwin, by stating that I became acquainted with you whilst living with Harriet, & that Godwin is the author of *Political Justice* & other *impious & seditious* writings.

I learn just now from Godwin that he has evidence that Harriet was unfaithful to me *four months* before I left England with you. If we can succeed in establishing this *our* connexion will receive an additional sanction, & plea be overborne.[26]

There are two versions of this letter among the family papers: the original and a forgery. Lady Shelley, who became hopelessly preoccupied with the details of Shelley's separation from Harriet and the extent of his culpability, muddled the two. She found a part of the forged copy in Mary Shelley's desk after her death, and assumed it to be genuine; the real letter she marked 'forgery'.

Figure 15 Portrait of Lord Byron, after George Sanders. Oxford, Bodleian Library, MS. Eng. misc. g. 181.

Exile

At the end of January 1818, a few weeks before the departure of Shelley, Mary and Claire Clairmont for the Continent, Godwin wrote a letter to Shelley in which he expressed his wish to revert to the philosophic spirit of their earlier letters to each other:

> I am ashamed of the tone I have taken with you in all our late conversations. I have played the part of a suppliant, & deserted that of a philosopher. It was not thus I talked with you, when I first knew you; & I will talk so no more. I will talk principles; I will talk Political Justice; whether it makes for me or against me, no matter. … I have nothing to say to you of a passionate nature; least of all, do I wish to move your feelings; less than the least, to wound you. All that I have to say, is in the calmness of philosophy, & moves far above the atmosphere of vulgar sensations.[27]

But their subsequent correspondence proved to be fitful and unbalanced. Godwin regularly sent letters to Italy, mostly addressed to Mary. Shelley wrote infrequently, and eventually stopped writing to Godwin altogether. In August 1820 he wrote to Godwin from Pisa advising him that he 'ought not to depend on me for any further pecuniary assistance at the present moment', and informing him that he was intercepting any letters that concerned financial affairs:

la penna su la speranza di esere esaudita, mentre
con tutto il rispetto, e la profonda venerazione mi protesto
Di V.ra Eccellenza

Che fà il mio Amato Pappà? io sto
così bene, e tanto contenta che
non posso se non ringraziare il sem-
pre Caro mio Pappa che mi pro-
curò un tanto bene a cui imploro
la sua Benedizione, La sua Allegrina lo saluta di cuore.

Cappuccine Bagnacavallo 31 Luglio 1821
                    Sua Dev.ª Serva
          La Madre Sup.ª Cappne

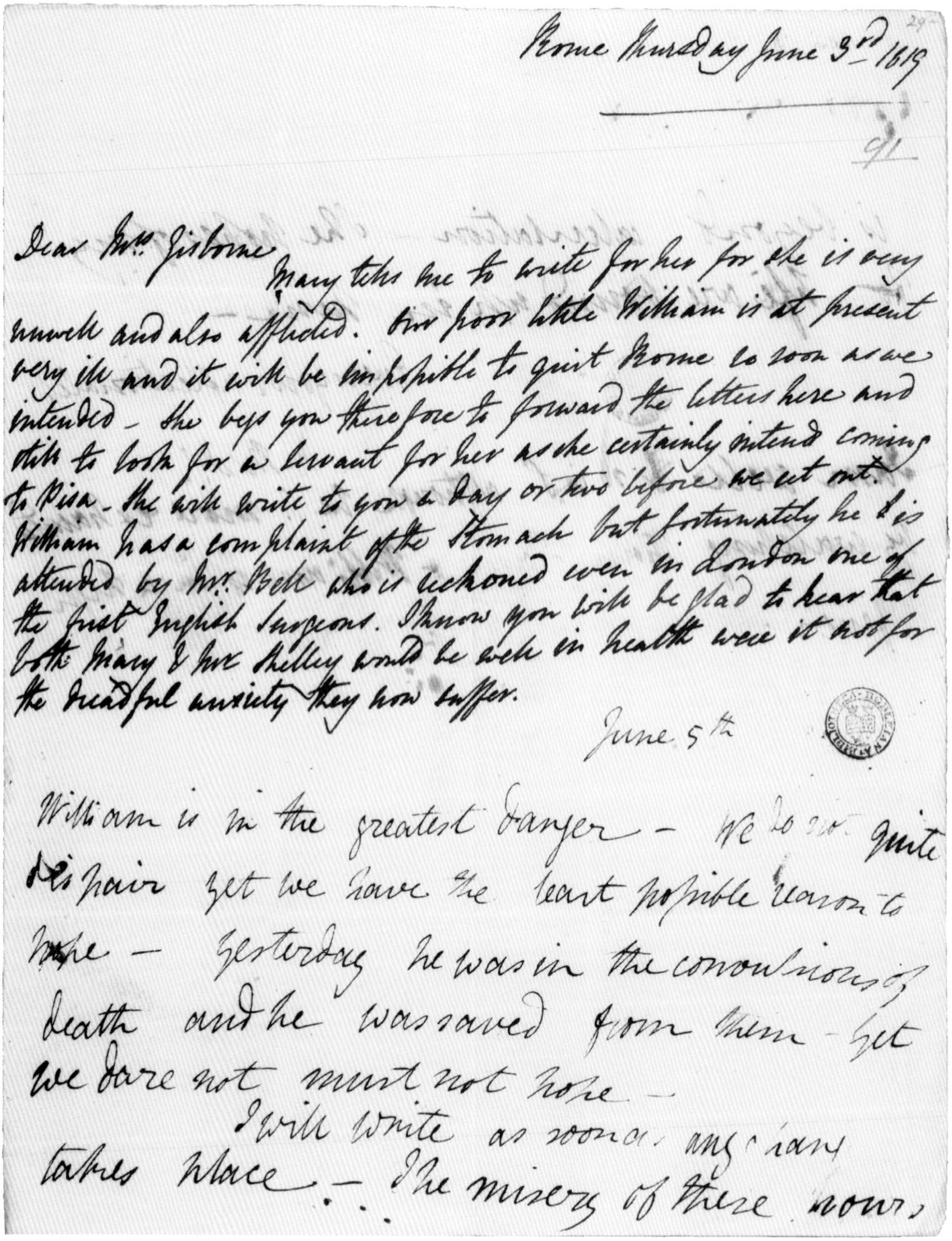

Rome Thursday June 3rd 1819

91

Dear Mrs Gisborne Mary tells me to write for her for she is very
unwell and also afflicted. Our poor little William is at present
very ill and it will be impossible to quit Rome so soon as we
intended — she begs you therefore to forward the letters here and
still to look for a servant for her as she certainly intends coming
to Pisa — she will write to you a day or two before we set out.
William has a complaint of the stomach but fortunately he is
attended by Mr Bell who is reckoned even in London one of
the first English surgeons. I know you will be glad to hear that
both Mary & Mr Shelley would be well in health were it not for
the dreadful anxiety they now suffer.

June 5th

William is in the greatest danger — We do not quite
despair yet we have the least possible reason to
hope — Yesterday he was in the convulsions of
death and he was saved from them — Yet
we dare not must not hope —
I will write as soon as any change
takes place — The misery of these hours

Figure 18 Letter from
Claire Clairmont and Mary
Shelley to Maria Gisborne,
3 and 5 June 1819 (death of
William). Oxford, Bodleian
Library, MS. Shelley c. 1,
fol. 292r.

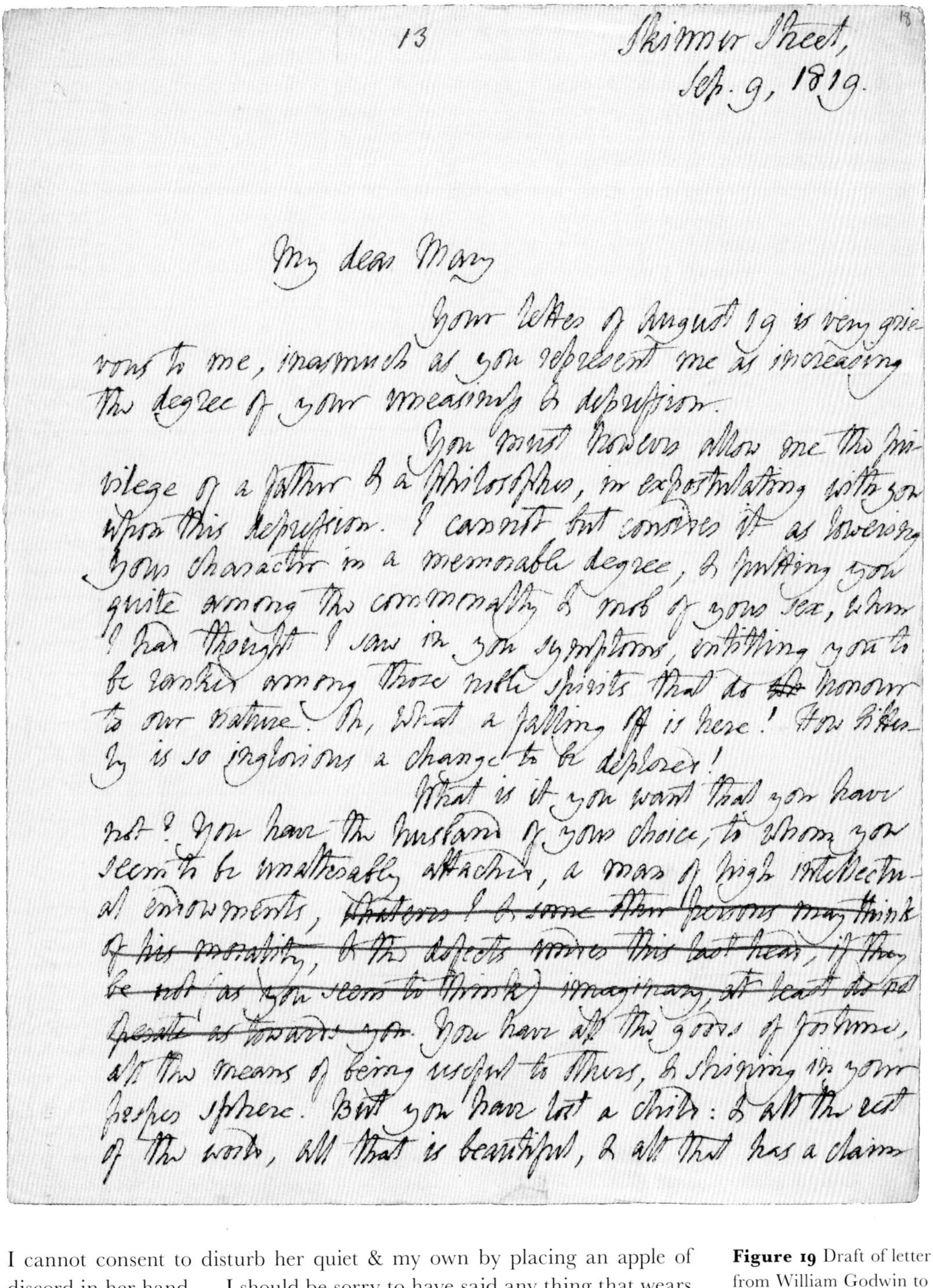

I cannot consent to disturb her quiet & my own by placing an apple of discord in her hand. … I should be sorry to have said any thing that wears the appearance of a threat; but imperious events compel me to foretell the consequences of your attempting to agitate her mind. I need not tell you that the neglecting entirely to write to your daughter from the moment than [*for* that] no money can be gained by it would admit of but one interpretation.[28]

Figure 19 Draft of letter from William Godwin to Mary Shelley, 9 September 1819. Written after William Shelley's death. Oxford, Bodleian Library, MS. Abinger c. 45, fol. 18r.

On receiving this letter Godwin allowed a rare show of emotion into his otherwise taciturn journal. 'Letter from Shelley', noted Godwin when he received this communication, then underlined the words.

Correspondence between Shelley and Mary in Italy is not extensive, and is naturally confined to periods when they were apart. Sometimes their letters touch upon the trials and tragedies of their years in exile. During the summer of their first year in Italy, while they were based at Bagni di Lucca, Shelley took Claire Clairmont to Venice, where her daughter Allegra was under Byron's care. Shelley wrote to Mary from Florence, giving her an account of their journey so far: 'Well my dearest Mary are you very lonely?' he asked her. 'Tell me truth my sweetest do you ever cry? I shall hear from you once at Venice & once on my return here'.[29] Five days later he wrote to her from Venice: Claire had seen Allegra, and he had seen Byron (who refused to see Claire). Thinking that Mary and Claire were in Padua, Byron had offered him the use of his summer house in nearby Este. Shelley now asked Mary to join him at Este: 'I have been obliged to decide on all these things without you. – I have done for the best & my own beloved Mary you must soon come & scold me if I have done wrong & kiss me if I have done right.'[30] Unknown to him, their infant daughter Clara was seriously ill; she died soon after the journey to Venice, a few weeks after her first birthday.

On hearing of Clara's death Godwin wrote a letter of sympathy to Mary, offering some dispassionate advice. After the death of the Shelleys' young son William in June the following year he wrote, again, as father and philosopher. He kept his original draft (with a deleted passage about Shelley) in his papers (Figure 19):

> Above all things I entreat you, do not put the miserable delusion upon yourself, to think there is something fine, & beautiful, & delicate, in giving yourself up, & agreeing to be nothing.
>
> Remember too that, though, at first, your nearest connections may pity you in this state, yet that when they see you fixed in sottishness & ill humour, & regardless of the happiness of every one else, they will finally cease to love you, & scarcely learn to endure you![31]

According to Lady Shelley, Mary was deeply upset by this 'hard, cruel letter'. 'Mary never got over that child's death', she told Maud Brooke, 'and even spoke of him just before her death. Godwin always thought of himself as an exalted being; he was hard and self-centred, but there was a faint likeness to Mary in his face, and when I notice that I cannot find it quite so hard. His daughter and grandson adored him, many revered him, though I never knew why! If Mary, his first wife, could have lived he would have been different; she died too soon, and you know, dear, the woman can make or mar the man!'[32]

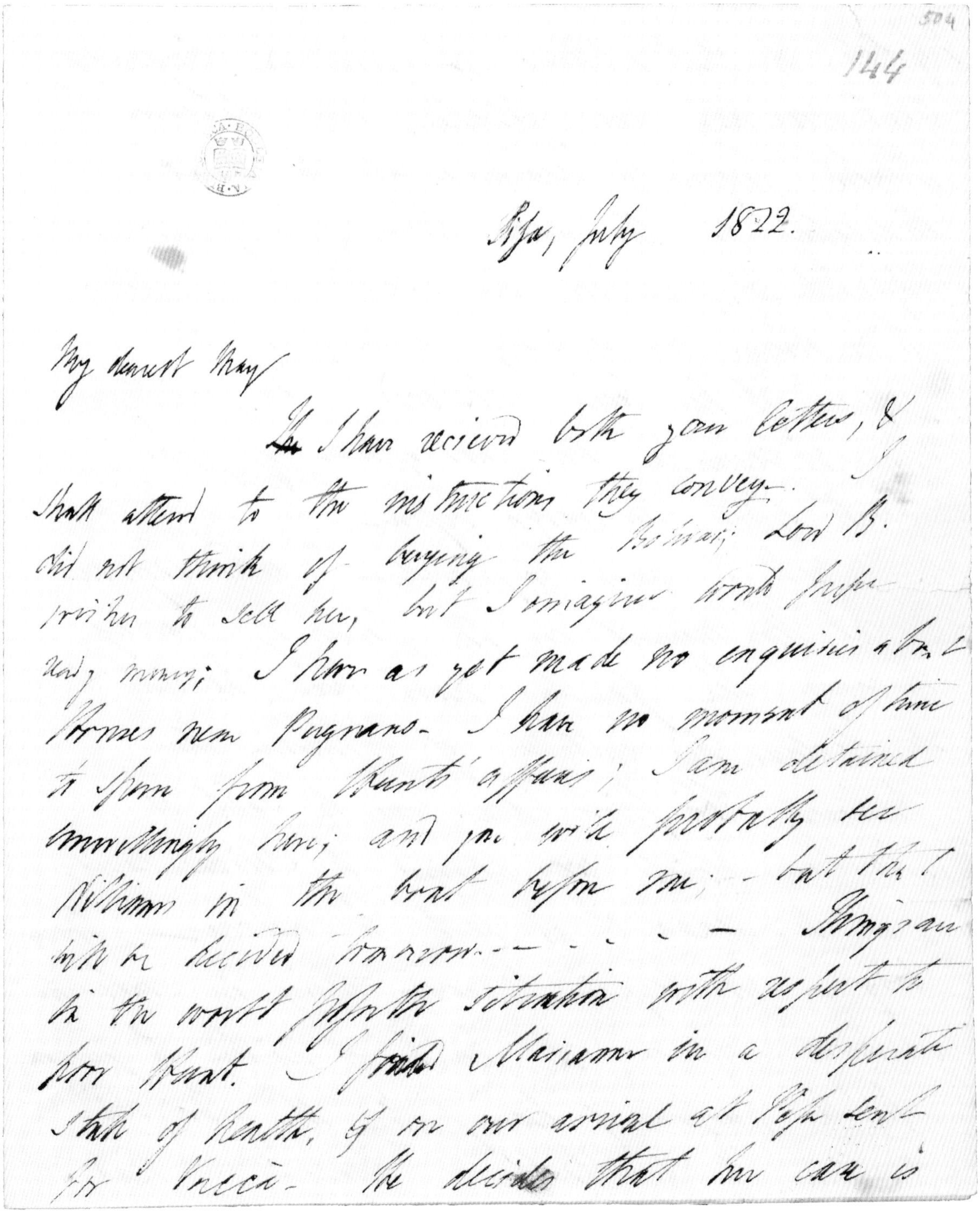
504

144

Pisa, July 1822.

My dearest Mary

I have received both your letters, & I shall attend to the instructions they convey. I did not think of buying the Bolivar; Lord B. wishes to sell her, but I imagine would prefer ready money. I have as yet made no enquiries about houses near Pugnano – I have no moment of time to spare from Hunt's affairs; I am detained unwillingly here, and you will probably see Williams in the boat before me, – but that will be decided tomorrow. – – – Thornton is in the worst possible situation with respect to poor Hunt. I found Marianne in a desperate state of health, & on our arrival at Pisa sent for Vacca – he decides that her case is

Figure 20 P.B. Shelley's last letter to Mary Shelley, 4 July 1822. Oxford, Bodleian Library, MS. Shelley c. 1, fol. 504r.

to-day, & am again disappointed. I shall hang in hope &
fear on every post, knowing that you cannot neglect me for
ever.

All that I expressed to you about si-
lence, & not writing to you again, is now put an end to
in the most melancholy way. I looked on you as one of the
daughters of prosperity, elevated in rank & fortune; & I
thought it was criminal to intrude on you for ever the
sorrows of an unfortunate old man & a beggar. You are
now fallen to my own level; & you are surrounded with ad-
versity & with difficulty; & I no longer hold it sacrilege
to trouble you with my adversities. We shall now truly sym-
pathise with each other; & whatever misfortune or ruin
falls upon me, I shall not now scruple to lay it fully before you.

This sorrowful event is perhaps calcula-
ted to draw us nearer to each other. I am the father of a family, but without children. I & my wife are falling fast into
infirmity & helplessness; &, in addition to all our other ca-
lamities, we seemed destined to be left without connections &
without aid. Perhaps now we and you shall mutually derive consolation p...

Poor Jane is I am afraid left still more
helpless than you are. Common misfortune I hope will excite
between you the most friendly feelings.

Shelley lived, I know, in constant
anticipation of the uncertainty of his life, though not in
this way; & was anxious in that event & to make the

In August 1821 Shelley travelled to Ravenna to see Byron, who wished to speak to him urgently about Allegra. Byron had refused to communicate directly with Claire Clairmont about their daughter: 'I should prefer hearing from you' he had told Shelley, 'as I must decline all correspondence with Claire who merely tries to be as irrational and provoking as she can be'.[33] He had placed Allegra in a convent, and had recently received a letter from the mother superior, with a childish note from 'la sua Allegrina' written underneath. The fact that this letter found its way into Shelley's papers[34] suggests that Byron gave it to him to show Claire. While in Ravenna Shelley learned that Byron's friends the Hoppners had been told a 'monstrous & incredible' story by the Shelleys' former servant Elise. He immediately wrote to Mary:

> Elise says that Clare was my mistress – that is all very well & so far there is nothing new: all the world has heard so much & people may believe or not believe as they think good. – She then proceeds to say that Clare was with child by me – that I gave her the most violent medicines to procure abortion – that this not succeeding she was brought to bed & that I immediately tore the child from her & sent it to the foundling hospital … In addition she says that both I & Clare treated *you* in the most shameful manner – that I neglected & beat you, & that Clare never let a day pass without offering you insults of the most violent kind in which she was abetted by me.[35]

The end of this letter is lost, and the remaining fragment was later subjected to heavy deletions. At Shelley's request Mary wrote to Mrs Hoppner refuting the story. 'Shocked beyond all measure as I was I instantly wrote the enclosed', she told Shelley. 'our bark is indeed tempest tost but love me as you have ever done & God preserve my child to me and our enemies shall not be too much for us.'[36]

With her words 'our bark is indeed tempest tost', Mary foretold the tragedy that would befall her the following summer. On 1 July 1822 Shelley and a friend, Edward Williams, sailed in Shelley's boat, the *Don Juan*, across the Bay of Spezia to Livorno to see Leigh Hunt. On their return journey seven days later a storm blew up, and they were lost at sea. The day before Shelley had said to Hunt's wife Marianne: 'If I die tomorrow I have lived to be older than my father, I am ninety years of age.'[37] He was, in fact, a few days short of his thirtieth birthday. He last wrote to Mary on 4 July, four days before his death. This hurried, businesslike letter concludes tenderly: 'How are you my best Mary? Write especially how is your health & how your spirits are, & whether you are not more reconciled to staying at Lerici at least during the summer. You have no idea how I am hurried & occupied – I have not a moments leisure – but will write by next post – Ever dearest Mary Yours affectionately, S.'[38] Mary's reply is a heavily damaged fragment, and may well have been with Shelley on his fatal voyage home.

On hearing of Shelley's death, Godwin wrote to his daughter his third letter of condolence in four years (Figure 21). He suggested that, after the recent storms, the tragedy might bring them back together: 'I suppose you will hardly stay in Italy. In that case we will be near to, & support each other.'[39]

The poet and the man

Contained within Shelley's correspondence are records of the most difficult and painful episodes of his short life: his early radicalism and tangled relationship with Godwin; his separation from Harriet and elopement with Mary; the suicides of Harriet and Fanny Imlay; the loss of Clara and William in Italy and Mary's subsequent depression; and his relationship with Claire Clairmont. Anyone interested in the poet could draw upon these documents and interpret them in their own way. To what extent was Shelley responsible for Harriet's, even Fanny's, suicide? Did his restless wandering around Italy hasten the deaths of his children? What was the precise nature of his relationship with Claire, and did it contribute to Mary's depression and loneliness? Anticipating, and fearing, this interest in Shelley's life, Lady Shelley did what she could to shape the family's reputation by guarding these letters closely and withholding them from all but a favoured few. Nearly all the letters of Shelley and Mary which she could identify ended up in the restricted box she presented to the Bodleian in 1893. They were not just family heirlooms and valuable literary documents; they were evidence.

'The Poet & the man are two different natures' wrote Shelley to his friends John and Maria Gisborne on 19 July 1821; 'though they exist together they may be unconscious of each other, & incapable of deciding upon each other's powers & effects by any reflex act'. As to whether or not *he* was a poet, he went on, this decision was 'removed from the present time to the hour when our posterity shall assemble: but the court is a very severe one, & I fear that the verdict will be guilty death'.[40] The court of posterity has indeed tried Shelley the poet; and another, equally severe court has assembled on numerous occasions to try Shelley the man, and delivered its verdict.

✣ 4 ✣

Shelley's Notebooks

'this jingling food for the hunger of oblivion'

If the letters in the family papers provide posterity with evidence of Shelley's character, then his achievement as a writer is preserved in his surviving notebooks.

As a young man Shelley expected to follow his father into Parliament, where he could impugn tyranny in its various forms (political, religious and sexual) and promote his belief in free speech, reason and human equality. But in his early letters to Godwin, written before he came of age, he admitted that he was not prepared to wait, and said that he would, in the meantime, express his beliefs in writing. He rejected the philosopher's warning against early publication: 'I publish, because I will publish nothing that shall not conduce to virtue, and therefore my publications so far as they do influence shall influence to good.'[1] So he employed his pen and the printing press to promote his cause, writing, publishing and handing out pamphlets and broadsides around Britain regardless of the risk. His servant, Dan Healy, even got imprisoned for distributing his *Declaration of Rights*. At the time such pamphlets suffered a precarious fate, and Shelley's youthful polemics are now rare and highly sought after. His friend Thomas Hookham, however, carefully held on to the copies Shelley gave him, and in 1858 presented them to the poet's son Sir Percy: *The Necessity of Atheism* (1811), *A Letter to Lord Ellenborough* (1812, one of only two known copies), and the two pamphlets Shelley published in Ireland, *An Address to the Irish People* and *Proposals for an Association of Philanthropists*.[2] These, together with the proof sheets, bearing Shelley's manuscript corrections, of a later pamphlet, *A Proposal for Putting Reform to the Vote Throughout the Kingdom* (1817),[3] were given to the Bodleian by Lady Shelley in 1893. Shelley was also, as he put it to Godwin, 'something of a Poet'. In 1812 he privately printed and distributed his first poem of any length, *Queen Mab*, which captured in verse the indignation and idealism of the pamphlets. Extensive notes protested the evils of, among other things, religion, marriage and meat-eating.

Figure 22 *p. 61* Five of
P.B. Shelley's notebooks.
Oxford, Bodleian Library.
Photo: Nick Cistone.

Shelley's personal actions and political commitments prevented him from taking his place in Parliament and left him an outsider and, ultimately, an exile. His early hopes of using the family fortune for philanthropic ends also went unfulfilled. He therefore turned to poetry. Occasionally he expressed doubts about its efficacy and viability. In the autumn of 1821, for instance, worried about money, he asked his friend Thomas Love Peacock about employment possibilities in India. Peacock, who worked at India House, had to tell him that such jobs were only open to life employees of the East India Company. In January the following year Shelley sent Peacock copies of his two latest publications, *Adonais*, an elegy on John Keats, and *Hellas*, a poem written in support of the Greeks in their struggle for independence from Turkey. 'I wish I had something better to do than furnish this jingling food for the hunger of oblivion, called *verse*', he wrote, 'but I have not, & since you give me no encouragement about India I cannot hope to have.'[4] Such doubts were, however, more than matched by his conviction that poetry was one of the greatest – perhaps *the* greatest – force in civilized life. It was a conviction that he would radiantly express in his 1821 essay, *A Defence of Poetry*, with its justly celebrated definition of poets as 'the unacknowledged legislators of the world'.

After *Queen Mab* Shelley published seven volumes under his name, and two anonymously. These volumes avoid the clear-cut opinions of the early political pamphlets in favour of a more ambivalent and questioning attitude. *Alastor*, published in 1816, is a long poem in blank verse that both celebrates and warns against the imaginative richness of solitude. *History of a Six Weeks' Tour*, Shelley and Mary's account of their visits to the Continent, published in 1817, includes two of his finest short poems, both written in Switzerland in 1816, *Mont Blanc* and *Hymn to Intellectual Beauty*. The former contemplates the relationship of the mind to the seeming indifference of nature, and ends on a note of questioning:

Mont Blanc yet gleams on high: – the power is there,
The still and solemn power of many sights,
And many sounds, and much of life and death.
In the calm darkness of the moonless nights,
In the lone glare of day, the snows descend
Upon that Mountain; none beholds them there,
Nor when the flakes burn in the sinking sun,
Or the star-beams dart through them: – Winds contend
Silently there, and heap the snow with breath
Rapid and strong, but silently! Its home
The voiceless lightning in these solitudes
Keeps innocently, and like vapour broods

Over the snow. The secret strength of things
Which governs thought, and to the infinite dome
Of heaven is as a law, inhabits thee!
And what were thou, and earth, and stars, and sea,
If to the human mind's imaginings
Silence and solitude were vacancy?

At the end of 1817 Shelley published his longest poem, *Laon and Cythna*, later revised and retitled *The Revolt of Islam*, which he described in a preface as 'an experiment on the temper of the public mind, as to how far a thirst for a happier condition of moral and political society survives, among the enlightened and refined, the tempests which have shaken the age in which we live.' The events of the poem are clearly derived from the French Revolution, and the relationship of the central figures, Laon and Cythna, offers a hope for the future. In the original version of the poem this relationship was incestuous.

Shelley continued to publish after leaving for Italy: *Rosalind and Helen*, a poem completed in England, was published in 1819. That year he also published a tragic play, *The Cenci*, and in 1820 his great epic drama *Prometheus Unbound*. Included with the latter were a number of poems which are now among Shelley's best known: *Ode to the West Wind*, *The Sensitive Plant*, *The Cloud*, *To a Skylark* and *Ode to Liberty*. In 1820 Shelley also published, anonymously, *Oedipus Tyrannus, or Swellfoot the Tyrant*, a burlesque attack on the government that was almost immediately withdrawn through fear of prosecution. *Epipsychidion* followed in 1821, also anonymously. Finally come the two books he sent to Peacock: *Adonais*, published in 1821, and *Hellas*, which appeared in early 1822.

Shelley published with a purpose. He had, he acknowledged in the preface to *Prometheus Unbound*, a 'passion for reforming the world'. 'But', he continued,

> it is a mistake to suppose that I dedicate my poetical compositions solely to the direct enforcement of reform, or that I consider them in any degree as containing a reasoned system on the theory of human life. Didactic poetry is my abhorrence; nothing can be equally well expressed in prose that is not tedious and supererogatory in verse. My purpose has hitherto been simply to familiarize the highly refined imagination of the more select classes of poetical readers with beautiful idealisms of moral excellence; aware that until the mind can love, and admire, and trust, and hope, and endure, reasoned principles of moral conduct are seeds cast upon the highway of life which the unconscious passenger tramples into dust, although they would bear the harvest of his happiness.

And I lay struggling with the impotence
Of sleep.. while outward life had burst its bound—
yet deluded, strove the tortured sense
To its dire wanderings, to adapt the sound
Which in the light of morn was poured around
Our dwelling;
breathless, pale & unaware
Rose, and all the cottage crowded round
With armed men, whose glittering swords were bare
whose degraded limbs the tyrants garb did wear

In *Prometheus Unbound* Shelley magnificently expressed his idealism and his lasting hope for a utopian way of life, but also a dejection and introspection, and an awareness of continual historical change, that are absent from his early writing. He offers no easy answers. The verse itself is so intricate as to be, on occasion, enigmatic; the imagery is abundant and dense, and the range of lyrical forms almost bewildering. Shelley is a challenging poet, and in his lifetime he was little read. A year after his death his publisher, Charles Ollier, sent Mary Shelley a list of unsold stock. 'The sale, in every instance, of Mr Shelley's works', he told her, 'has been very confined.'[5] Despite its difficulties, however, Shelley's work has proved to be endlessly rewarding. Much of it remained unpublished and incomplete at his death, hidden away in his numerous private notebooks. The richness and complexity of this unpublished work has only recently been fully investigated and appreciated.

'a dozen plain books'

In February 1820 Mary Shelley wrote to Maria Gisborne from Pisa asking her for a number of hard-to-find items: 'a good Quarto Bible', two or three small combs, and 'some Arrow root, or in default of that Tapioca'. She adds a final request: 'Would you have the kindness to order at your Stationers a dozen plain books like that the Prometheus was copied in. I think the price was three pauls or more, but perhaps you or Beppe will remember'.[6] Shelley tended to throw things away, or at least not bother to keep track of where things were, but losing a literary manuscript distressed him, and he rarely, one imagines, travelled without at least one of his notebooks. At least one of them now shows signs of water damage, and may have been with Shelley on his final voyage, stowed away in the trunk that was salvaged from the wreck of his boat, the *Don Juan*.

The Shelleys purchased their blank books either singly, or, as Mary's letter to Maria Gisborne shows, in bulk. Once purchased, they would then be picked up or laid aside, according to the needs or whims of the moment; some might lie unused for years. While a notebook was in use, pages might be torn from it as a quick source of blank paper, or to get rid of poorly regarded or potentially confusing drafts. Nearly all the notebooks have suffered in this way. Shelley almost never wrote in only one notebook at a time, systematically filling it and then moving on to another. Instead, he often used two or more notebooks concurrently, and might put one aside for a time, only to return to it later. Spaces were filled up as occasion demanded. In addition, he would typically use both the front and end of the notebooks at the same time, working inwards towards the middle. Snatches from several works are mixed together on

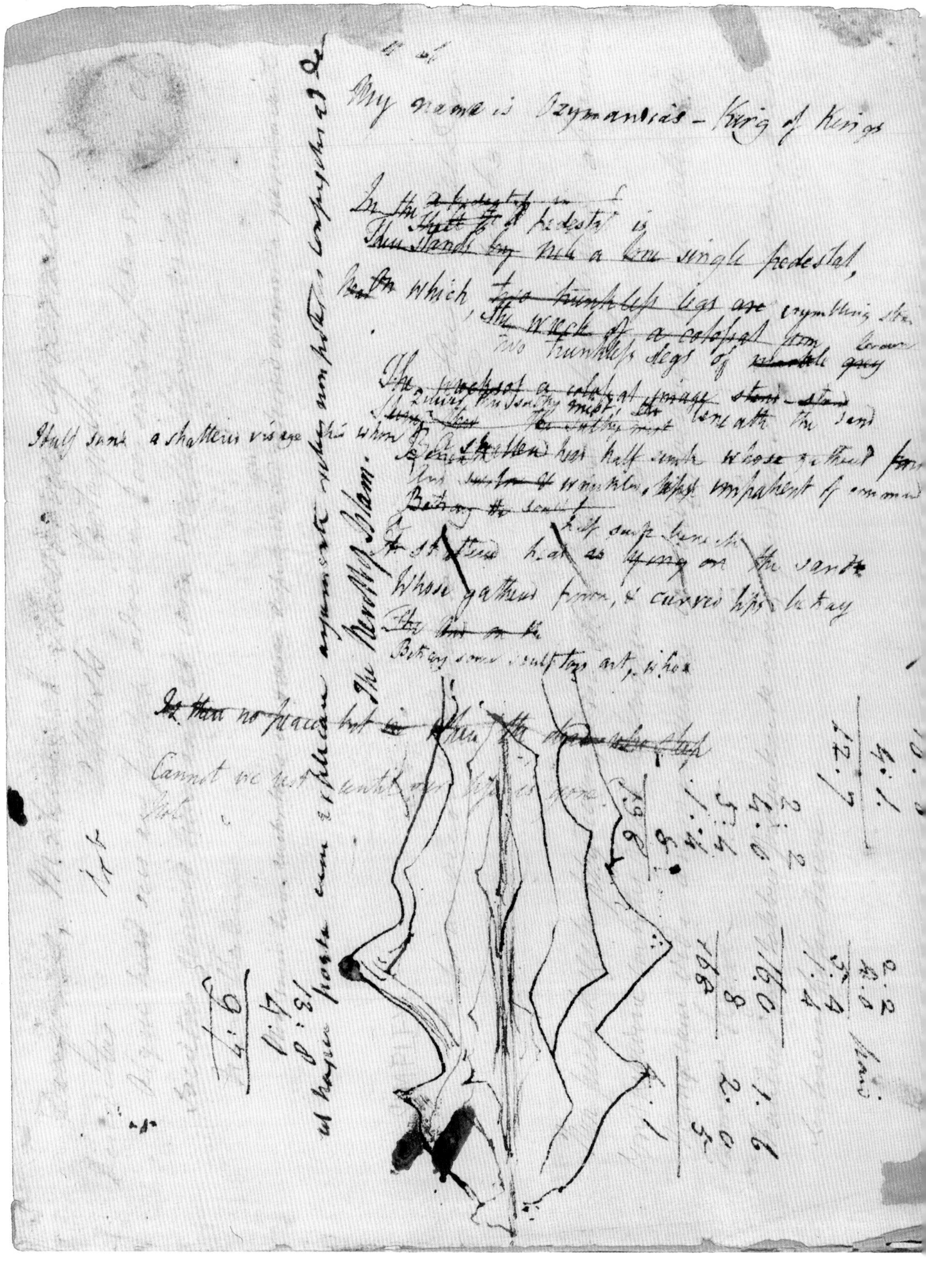

My name is Ozymandias — King of Kings

In the [...]
Thou [...] a pedestal is
There stands by me a [bare] single pedestal,

On which [...] the trunkless legs are crumbling the
the wreck of a colossal [...]
two trunkless legs of [...] grey

[...] of a colossal image stand
[...] beneath the sand

Itself sans a shatter'd visage whose [...]
Near it stretched lies half sunk whose gathered brow
And wrinkles [...] imperious of command

A shatter'd head is lying on the sand
Whose gathered brow, & curved lips betray

But its some sculptres art, who

Is there no peace but [...]

Cannot we not until [...]

[sketch and scattered figures/numbers]

the same page, while individual poems thread their way fitfully, and in seemingly random order, through one or more notebooks.

The various poems, prose pieces and fragments are anything from initial drafts to intermediate fair copies. Mixed up with literary composition are reading notes, memoranda, draft letters, accounts, and the numerous doodles, typically of trees or sailing boats, that Shelley habitually drew during intervals of thought. Sometimes he adorned the covers of the notebook with such drawings.

Figure 24 P.B. Shelley, draft of *Ozymandias*. Oxford, Bodleian Library, MS. Shelley e. 4, fol. 85v.

Figure 25 P.B. Shelley, draft of *Julian and Maddalo*. Oxford, Bodleian Library, MS. Shelley adds. e. 11, p. 65.

Figure 26 P.B. Shelley, draft of *Ode to the West Wind*. Oxford, Bodleian Library, MS. Shelley adds. c. 12, p. 63.

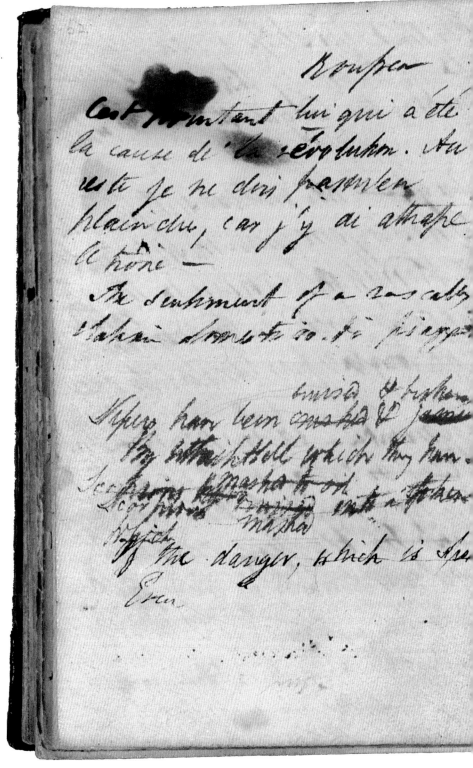

Oct. 25

O wild West Wind thou breath of Autumn's being

Thou, from whose unseen presence the leaves dead

Are driven, like ghosts from an enchanter fleeing

Yellow & black & pale & hectic red

Pestilence-stricken multitudes — o Thou

Who chariotest to their dark wintry bed

The winged seeds, where they lie cold & low

Each like a corpse within its grave, until

Thine azure sister of the Spring shall blow

Her clarion oer the dreaming earth, & fill

~~The~~ ~~vacant depth of the~~

~~& no doleful~~

~~all wreathing~~

~~Driving sweet buds like flocks to fix in air~~

~~In the vacant space of the~~

With living hues & odours plain & hill

Wild Spirit which art moving everywhere

Destroyer & Preserver, hear a hear

And other whiles the lady

When the moon was in the
wan
In the noon of winter nights

Her spirit, but she sailed forth under the
Of shooting stars,

Where like a meadow which in scythe has
Of rain had been bent, or wind had shaven

With the Antarctic
Which had never bent & c[ould] shake
With the Antarctic constellations heaven

And the youth her self a wind less haven
Out of the clouds where moving
The Spirit of the tempest

Figure 27 *left* P.B. Shelley, draft of *The Witch of Atlas*. MS. Shelley adds. e. 6, p. 85 rev.

Figure 28 *above* P.B. Shelley, sketches of sailing boats. Oxford, Bodleian Library, MS. Shelley adds. e. 18, p. 106 rev.

'an idealized history of my life and feelings'

Shelley filled his notebooks in a way that had to make sense only to himself. Even Mary, who knew his handwriting and literary processes as well as anyone, found it immensely difficult to decipher them after his death. Other readers, more or less expert, have laboured over the notebooks since then and found them no less challenging, but few have ever concluded that the labour had not been worth it. For behind the apparent chaos of the pages are distinct patterns. Expert analysis – of the physical structure of the notebooks, of the types of ink, the various states of Shelley's nib, the biographical, historical and literary contexts – can piece a poem together across notebooks, trace the relationships of its various drafts and build chronologies.

The notebooks reveal the richness and variety of Shelley's intellectual life. Beyond a few domestic memoranda, they are free of quotidian details. Instead they show a highly experimental and literary mind at work, disciplining and shaping its thoughts and imaginings to create self-sufficient poetry and prose. They offer a kind of antidote to the controversies and emotional upheavals of the letters and journals, forming the heart of the family archive and at the same time standing aloof from it. Lady Shelley never fretted over the contents of the notebooks in the way she did with the letters. In a prose draft ('On Learning Languages'), first published as a letter to an unnamed woman, Shelley wrote:

> Facts are not what we want to know in poetry, in history, in the lives of individual men, in satire, or in panegyric. They are the mere divisions, the arbitrary points on which we hang, and to which we refer those delicate and evanescent hues of mind, which language delights and instructs us in precise proportion as it expresses.[7]

What is more, Shelley believed that art neither explains or excuses the transgressions of the life. Posterity judged the poet and the man in different courts. He wrote in *A Defence of Poetry*:

> Let us assume that Homer was a drunkard, that Virgil was a flatterer, that Horace was a coward, that Tasso was a madman, that Lord Bacon was a peculator, that Raphael was a libertine, that Spenser was a poet laureate. Their errors have been weighed and found to have been dust in the balance; if their sins 'were as scarlet, they are now as white as snow': they have been washed in the blood of the mediator and redeemer, time. Observe in what a ludicrous chaos the imputations of real or fictitious crime have been confused in the contemporary calumnies against poetry and poets; consider how little is, as it appears – or appears, as it is; look to your own motives, and judge not, lest ye be judged.

Mary Shelley was the first person to tackle the complexities of the notebooks after Shelley's death. She approached them above all as a literary editor. In her 1839 edition of Shelley's poems she divided his poetry into two classes, 'the purely imaginative, and those which sprang from the emotions of his heart':

> The second class is, of course, the more popular, as appealing at once to emotions common to us all; some of these rest on the passion of love; others on grief and despondency; others on the sentiments inspired by natural objects. Shelley's conception of love was exalted, absorbing, allied to all that is purest and noblest in our nature, and warmed by earnest passion; such it appears when he gave it a voice in verse. Yet he was usually averse to expressing these feelings, except when highly idealized; and many of his more beautiful effusions he had cast aside unfinished, and they were never seen by me till after I had lost him.

Epipsychidion is perhaps Shelley's finest expression of his exalted conception of love. He composed the poem from late 1820 to early 1821. It was published, anonymously, later that year. The title is constructed from the Greek words *epi* (upon) and *psychidion* (little soul). In the 'advertisement' with which he prefaced the published poem, Shelley wrote that the poem, 'like the *Vita Nuova* of Dante, is sufficiently intelligible to a certain class of readers without a matter-of-fact history of the circumstances to which it relates.' *Epipsychidion* has, nevertheless, often been read in the context of Shelley's matter-of-fact history. At the time of writing the poem he, Mary and Claire regularly visited and corresponded with Teresa Viviani, the nineteen-year-old daughter of the governor of Pisa, who was confined in a convent. *Epipsychidion* is addressed to 'Emilia V——, now imprisoned in the convent of ——'; the 'Emily' of the poem is the idealized object of the poet's love:

> Poor captive bird! Who, from thy narrow cage,
> Pourest such music, that it might assuage
> The rugged hearts of those who prisoned thee,
> Were they not deaf to all sweet melody;
> This song shall be thy rose: its petals pale
> Are dead, indeed, my adored Nightingale!
> But soft and fragrant is the faded blossom,
> And it has no thorn left to wound thy bosom.   (ll. 5–12)

In a passage which can be read as a commentary on his then strained relationship with Mary, Shelley contrasts his love for Emily with the dead state of marriage, one of the 'rocks on which high hearts are wreckt':

> I never was attached to that great sect,
> Whose doctrine is, that each one should select
> Out of the crowd a mistress or a friend,
> And all the rest, though fair and wise, commend
> To cold oblivion, though it is in the code
> Of modern morals, and the beaten road
> Which those poor slaves with weary footsteps tread,
> Who travel to their home among the dead
> By the broad highway of the world, and so
> With one chained friend, perhaps a jealous foe,
> The dreariest and the longest journey go.   (ll. 147–159)

In the central section of *Epipsychidion* the poet narrates his personal history, describing in a series of planetary images the 'many mortal forms' in which he sought 'The shadow of that idol of my thought'. One, the moon, has been read as Mary Shelley:

> One stood on my path who seemed
> As like the glorious shape which I had dreamed,
> As is the Moon, whose changes ever run
> Into themselves, to the eternal Sun;
> The cold chaste Moon, the Queen of Heaven's bright isles,
> Who makes all beautiful on which she smiles,
> That wandering shrine of soft yet icy flame
> Which ever is transformed, yet still the same,
> And warms not but illumines.   (ll. 277–85)

Contrasting with the cold light of the moon is the bright warmth of the sun that is Emily (and perhaps Teresa Viviani):

> Soft as an Incarnation of the Sun,
> When light is changed to love, this glorious One
> Floated into the cavern where I lay,
> And called my Spirit, and the dreaming clay
> Was lifted by the thing that dreamed below
> As smoke by fire, and in her beauty's glow
> I stood, and felt the dawn of my long night
> Was penetrating me with living light:
> I knew it was the Vision veiled from me
> So many years – that it was Emily.   (ll. 335–344)

The poet leaves the moon behind him and concludes with an ecstatic vision of the poet and Emily arriving at an island paradise.

Mary Shelley never spoke specifically about *Epipsychidion*, indeed it was the only major poem in her 1839 edition of Shelley's works which lacks an accompanying note. In the journal she started after the poet's death she seems to echo the sentiments of the poem: 'Oh my beloved

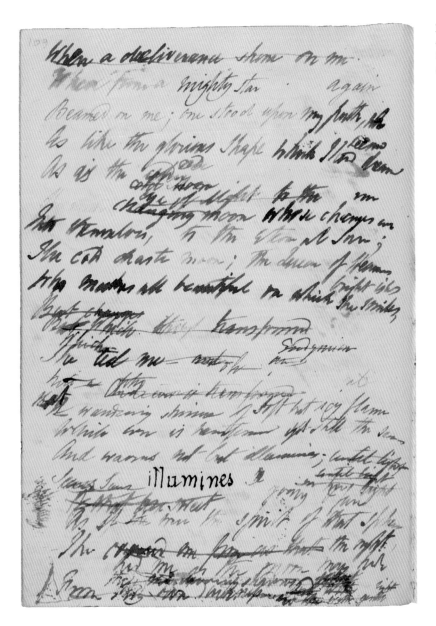

Figure 29 P.B. Shelley, draft of *Epipsychidion*. Oxford, MS. Shelley adds. e. 8, p. 109.

Shelley – It is not true that this heart was cold to thee.'[8] 'I am said to have a cold heart', she wrote to Byron in February 1823; 'there are feelings however so strongly implanted in my nature that to root them out life will go with it.'[9] Shelley himself seemed to fear that *Epipsychidion*, once published, would be taken as autobiographical. In February 1821 he sent the poem, together with the 'Ode to Naples' and a sonnet, to Charles Ollier for publication. He gave him particular instructions concerning *Epipsychidion*:

The longer poem, I desire, should not be considered as my own; indeed, in a certain sense, it is a production of a portion of me already dead; and in this sense the advertisement is no fiction. It is to be published simply for the esoteric few; and I make its author a secret, to avoid the malignity of those who turn sweet food into poison; transforming all they touch into the corruption of their own natures. My wish with respect to it is, that it should be printed immediately in the simplest form, and merely one hundred copies: those who are capable of judging and feeling rightly with respect to a composition of so abstruse a nature, certainly do not arrive at that number – among those, at least, who would ever be excited to read an obscure and anonymous production; and it should give me no pleasure that the vulgar should read it.[10]

Shelley soon changed his mind about publishing the poem at all, and asked Ollier to withdraw it. After his death Ollier told Mary Shelley that he still had 160 stitched copies in stock: 'As it was the wish of Mr Shelley that the whole of the "Epipsychidion" should be suppressed, I would not, though it was printed at our expense, suffer the remainder to be disposed of.'[11] A month before his death Shelley told John Gisborne that he could hardly bear to look at *Epipsychidion*: 'the person whom it celebrates was a cloud instead of a Juno … It is an idealized history of my life and feelings. I think one is always in love with something or other; the error, and I confess it is not easy for spirits cased in flesh and blood to avoid it, consists in seeking in a mortal image the likeness of what is perhaps eternal.'[12]

Whatever its biographical origins or indiscretions, however, *Epipsychidion* is entirely successful as a poem. Its rhyming couplets and unusual imagery brilliantly sustain a tension between clouds and Junos, the sensual and the spiritual, the physical and the abstract. The notebooks testify to the large amount of time Shelley spent conceiving, revising and refining the poem, and how it seemed to grow out of a confused mass of disparate fragments and other works. Characteristically, he did not start a notebook specifically for the poem, but wrote drafts for it and the 'advertisement' onto blank pages wherever he could find them. They are therefore spread over some five notebooks:

- A cheaply made pocket-book[13] of ruled English paper was used over a long period in England and Italy. Shelley also used it to draft 'Homeric Hymns', his unfinished prose tale 'The Coliseum', drafts of private lyrics, drafts of Acts II and IV of *Prometheus Unbound*, the start of an intermediate fair copy of *The Mask of Anarchy*, and drafts for *The Sensitive Plant*.
- The 'Devils notebook'[14] was used between November 1819 and October 1821. As well as scrappy reading notes and extracts from

Greek and other authors, it contains drafts for *On the Devil and Devils*, *Letter to Maria Gisborne* and *Adonais*.

𝄞 A notebook originally used by Mary Shelley[15], and then taken over by Shelley, may have been with Shelley on his last voyage. It includes a draft of the prose work *Speculation on Morals and Metaphysics* (part of a long work going back to 1814–15), an early draft of *A Defence of Poetry*, and intermediate fair copies of *The Witch of Atlas* and *Ode to Naples*.

𝄞 A sturdily made notebook[16] of Italian paper, now in a worn condition, was initially intended for the continuation of Shelley's work on his translation of Plato's *Symposium* in summer 1818, laid aside, and then taken up again from autumn 1819 for political songs and lyrics of 1819–20. Its contents include the second part of *A Discourse on the Manners of the Ancients* and the related *On the Symposium*; drafts for *Arethusa, Ode to Liberty, The Witch of Atlas, Ode to the West Wind, Liberty, Hymn of Apollo* and *Hymn of Pan* and *The Cloud*; and Shelley's reading notes taken in April 1820 from Sir Humphry Davy's *Elements of Agricultural Chemistry* (1812).

𝄞 A notebook,[17] probably bought at Bagni di Lucca in 1818, was used by Shelley mainly over one winter, 1820–21, in Pisa. As well as *Epipsychidion* it contains Shelley's drafts for 'Ode to Naples' and 'Swellfoot the Tyrant', a fragment of 'Adonais', a 'Dialogue on Keats' and his essays 'On the Punishment of Death' and *A Defence of Poetry*. *Epipsychidion* seems to have been developed from two poems drafted in this notebook, 'Fiordispina' and 'Ginevra'; indeed, it is not always possible to tell which lines belong to which poem. The notebook also contains Shelley's reading notes for, and partial translation of, Dante's *Convito* (Italian), his translation of parts of Calderon's *La Cisma de Ingalaterra* (Spanish), and translations of several Platonic epigrams (Greek).

Drafts for all but 195 lines of *Epipsychidion* can be traced in these notebooks, together with other lines not used in the published poem, some of which were later published as 'Fragments connected with *Epipsychidion*'. That Shelley was reading Dante (not only the *Convito* but, as Mary Shelley's journal records, the *Vita Nuova*) shows the immediate literary inspirations for the poem, and explains its formalized modes of expression and address. Having glimpsed the laborious process of the poem's composition in the notebooks, and the alchemy with which Shelley pulls together the various drafts and creates a finished poem, one can appreciate *Epipsychidion* not so much as an artful fragment of autobiography, but as an artful, and complete poem. One understands why William Wordsworth called Shelley 'one of the best artists of us all; I mean in workmanship of style'.

occupation. The leaves of that year were withered before my work drew near a close, and now every day shewed me more plainly how well I had succeeded. But my enthusiasm was checked by my ~~own~~ anxiety and I appeared rather like one doomed by slavery to toil in the mines or any other unwholsome trade than an artist occupied in his favourite employment. Every ~~night~~ night a slow fever ~~oppressed~~ me and I became nervous ~~nervous~~ to a ~~degree~~ most painful degree; a ~~fever~~ a disease I regretted ~~the~~ more because I had hitherto enjoyed excellent health & ~~my nerves~~ ~~were~~ ~~firm~~ had always boasted of ~~the~~ my firmness of my nerves. But I believed that exercise and amusement would soon ~~drive~~ drive away ~~these~~ such symptoms and I promised myself both of these when my creation should be ~~completed~~. ~~I had then~~ ~~determined to~~ ~~go to Geneva~~ ~~as soon as this should be~~ ~~done~~ ~~and~~ ~~in the midst of my~~ ~~family~~ ~~fond~~ ~~eve~~ —

Chapter 7th

It was on a dreary night of November that I beheld ~~the frame on which~~ my man completed with an anxiety that almost ~~ed~~ to agony. I collected ~~instruments~~ around me ~~and endeavour~~ that I might infuse a spark of being into the lifeless ~~thing~~ that lay at my feet. It was ~~already~~ one in the morning, the rain ~~pattered~~ dismally against the window ~~and~~ my candle was nearly burnt out, by the glimmer of the half exti ed light I saw the dull yellow eye ~~of~~ the creature open — It breathed ~~hard~~, and a convulsive motion agitated its limbs.

~~But how~~ ~~how~~ How can I describe emotion at this catastrophe, or ho eate the wretch whom with infinite pains and care I had en to form. His limbs were in proporti beautiful and I had selected his features ~~handsome~~ ~~Handsome~~. ~~Beautiful~~. Handsome; great God yellow ~~skin~~ skin scarcely covered the wo muscles and arteries beneath; his ha of a lustrous black, & was flowing and his teeth of a pearl ness but these luxuriances only f formed a more horrid contrast his watry eyes that seemed almo the same colour as the dun whi sockets in which they were se

5

Frankenstein

'Mary was there. Shelley was also with me.'

Who wrote *Frankenstein*? It was a question people must have asked themselves when the novel first appeared at the beginning of 1818, anonymously, and dedicated to William Godwin. Today the story is part of popular culture; then it was startlingly new. Walter Scott described it as 'peculiar'; John Croker found it 'horrible and disgusting'.[1] After days of obsessive and solitary study a young student of natural philosophy, Victor Frankenstein, discovers how to give life to inert matter. Using body parts taken from charnel houses, he succeeds in creating a being of monstrous size and dreadful appearance. The creature is condemned to a life of solitude and hiding, and comes to hate his creator. Over the course of the novel he destroys everyone dear to Frankenstein: his younger brother William, his closest friend Clerval, and his bride Elizabeth. But Frankenstein refuses to grant the creature's request for a female counterpart, and pursues him to the Arctic. There he encounters an English explorer, Walton, and dies after telling him his story. The creature comes to see Frankenstein's corpse, and tells Walton that he will continue to the far north, and there destroy himself.

In Godwin's earlier novel *St. Leon*, an aristocrat learns the secret of eternal life. His discovery alienates him from his family and friends, and eventually deprives him of his humanity. 'Frankenstein is a novel upon the same plan with Saint Leon', wrote Scott in *Blackwoods Edinburgh Magazine*; 'it is said to be written by Mr Percy Bysshe Shelley, who, if we are rightly informed, is son-in-law to Mr Godwin; and it is inscribed to that ingenious author.' No one could then have deduced that the novel was the work not of Godwin's son-in-law, but of his twenty-year-old daughter Mary. Shelley did not write *Frankenstein*. His name, nevertheless, has remained attached to the novel, and the precise nature and extent of his contribution has often been debated.

In 1875, when pressed to provide information about Shelley and Mary, Claire Clairmont commented on the intellectual character of

Mary did not know our danger. She was resting on
my knees that were unable to support her. She did
not speak or look. But I felt that she was there.
I had time in that moment to reflect & even to
reason upon death. It was rather a thing of
discomfort & of disapointment than sorrow to
me. We should never be separated, but in death
we might not know & feel our union as now.
I hope — but my hopes are not unmixed with fear
for what will befall this inestimable spirit when
we appear to die.

The morning broke, the lightning died away, the
violence of the wind abated. We arrived at Calais
whilst Mary still slept. We drove upon the sand.
Suddenly the broad sun rose over France.
France. ~~Thursday~~ Friday. 29
I said — Mary look. The sun rises over France.
We walked over the sands to the Inn. We we
shewn into an apartment that ~~answered~~ the
purpose both of a sitting & sleeping room.
Mary was there. Shelley was also with m

In the evening Captain Davison came & told us
that a fat lady had arrived, who had said th
I had ran away with her daughter. It wa
Mrs. Godwin. ~~&~~ Jane spent the night wi

their relationship. It was not Harriet's fault, she said, that Shelley had left her for Mary: 'he fell desperately in love with Mary, who had great understanding and both knowledge and liking for the abstract subjects and high thoughts he delighted in – this, poor Harriet had not – she was only a beautiful accomplished school girl extremely fond of her husband'.[2] Shelley and Mary's elopement in 1814 may have estranged them from Godwin, but his marriage with Mary Wollstonecraft remained, for the young couple, an exemplary intellectual partnership. Their reading in 1814 included Godwin's *Political Justice* and *Caleb Williams*, and Mary Wollstonecraft's *Letters Written during a Short Residence in Sweden, Norway, and Denmark*, together with her *Mary, a Fiction* and *The Wrongs of Woman, or Maria*. Shared reading remained an important part of their relationship in Italy. On July 1818 Shelley wrote to Thomas Love Peacock from Bagni di Lucca, describing how he would sit on the rocks reading Herodotus, then dive into a pool of cold, transparent water. He was, he told Peacock, reading only Greek, 'and a little Italian poetry with Mary. We have finished Ariosto together – a thing I could not have done again alone.'[3] Other authors Shelley and Mary read together include Aeschylus, Boccaccio, Cervantes, Coleridge, Dante, Gibbon, Horace, Keats, Montaigne, Shakespeare, Sophocles, Virgil, Voltaire and Wordsworth.

Shelley and Mary's literary collaboration is recorded in a number of notebooks and loose papers. During their elopement they purchased a notebook in Paris to serve as their jointly maintained journal. Shelley made the first few entries; at the end of his description of their arrival in France Mary took his pen and completed his entry. It is easy to say exactly where she took over:

> France Friday. 29
>   I said – Mary look. The sun rises over France.
>   We walked over the sands to the Inn. We were shewn into an apartment that answered the purpose both of a sitting & sleeping room. Mary was there. S.helley was also with me [4]

Mary soon took over the journal completely. Her entry for 25 August 1814, made when they had reached Lake Lucerne, reads: 'We arrange our apartments – & write part of Shelleys Romance.' The romance was the prose tale *The Assassins*; the loose leaves on which it was written have survived, and are among the earliest literary manuscripts in the archive. Sometimes the handwriting is Shelley's as he drafts the text, sometimes it is Mary's, as she takes down his dictation, perhaps offering a few suggestions of her own. A more light-hearted example of the two of them sharing the page can be seen in a pocketbook kept by Shelley during their years in Italy. They are playing *bouts-rimés*, a popular

Figure 31 P.B. Shelley and Mary Shelley, joint journal entry for 29 July 1814. Oxford, Bodleian Library, MS. Abinger d. 27, fol. 2r.

parlour game in which couples challenged each other with rhyming words. Mary supplies the rhymes (shown here in italics) and challenges Shelley to develop them into meaningful lines of verse:

> By the everl[a]sting *God*
> It seems to me extremely *odd*
> That in Hell forever *burning*
> And the Holy Ghost's grace *spurning*
> And the Virgin Mary's *flower*,
> Ever longing to *devour*
> Thou should'st, in thy dreadful *sorrow*,
> Never steal or beg or *borrow*
> Any of the bright lamps *seven*
> Burning before God [in?] *Heaven*.

Below this are draft lines from Shelley's poem *The Sensitive Plant*.

Shelley's notebooks, discussed in the previous chapter, retain marks of this collaborative literary and intellectual life. A number of hands occasionally break into the poet's solitary imaginings, belonging, for example, to Leigh Hunt, who sketched ideas into one notebook for the next issue of the *Liberal* magazine, either shortly before or, more likely, shortly after the poet's sudden death. But by far the most common hand is that of Mary.

Notebooks passed between Shelley and Mary continually. Mary, used one for a month to keep the household accounts at Marlow; Shelley later picked it up in Italy and, starting from the other end, used it mainly to draft his poem *Peter Bell the Third*. Another contains Mary's drafts for *The Fields of Fancy* and the start of its revision, *Mathilda*, both dating from 1819, and then a number of Shelley's later drafts, including lines for *Epipsychidion* and parts of *A Defence of Poetry*. In another, Mary has written notes on the story of the Cenci family in Rome, which Shelley was suggesting she turn into a tragedy. She made an English translation of *Relazione della morte della Famiglia Cenci*, to which Shelley made a number of corrections. He would later write the tragedy himself. Shelley also wrote a number of his verses into this notebook, but later tore the pages out. It contains the remnants of a sketch that may be by Shelley, or possibly by Mary. The family papers also show evidence of Mary's role as Shelley's secretary or amanuensis: a number of them contain her fair copies of his poems.

'a juvenile attempt of mine'

The manuscript that reveals the most about the collaborative nature of Shelley and Mary's relationship is the first full draft of *Frankenstein*.

Figure 32 P.B. Shelley, view across Lake Geneva. Oxford, Bodleian Library, MS. Shelley adds. c. 4, fol. 71v.

Famously, the idea for the novel was conceived in the summer of 1816, while Shelley, Mary and Claire Clairmont were staying in Geneva as the guests of Lord Byron. Byron's doctor, John Polidori, was also with them. Wet weather kept them indoors, and at Byron's suggestion they all, with the exception of Claire, tried their hands at a ghost story. Shelley soon gave his up. Byron began a story but quickly became bored, and Polidori's story *The Vampyre* was eventually published, anonymously, in 1819 (for a while people thought it was by Byron). Mary Shelley came up with *Frankenstein*.

According to Mary's later account, the idea came to her in a dream, of which she wrote a brief transcript. The manuscript of this has been lost. Mary Shelley then took a large notebook, most probably one that she had purchased in Geneva specially for the purpose, and began a longer, two-volume version of the story. 'Shelley & I talk about my story', she wrote in her journal on 21 August 1816.[5] She continued to work on the novel on their return to England, and on 5 December 1816 wrote to Shelley from Bath: 'I have also finished the 4 Chap. of Frankenstein which is a very long one & I think you would like it'.[6] At around this time she ran out of blank pages, and purchased a second

We had arrived in England at the beginning of October and it was now february; we also determined to commence our journey towards the north at & at the expiration another month. In this expedition we did not intend to follow the great road to Edinburgh But to visit windsor, oxford, matlock & cumberland lakes resolving to arrive at completion of this tour about the end of July. I packed my chemical instruments & the materials which I had collected meaning to finish my labours in some obscure nook in the country.

We quitted London on the 27 of march and remained a few days at windsor rambling in its beautiful forest. This was a new scene to us mountaineers; the majestic oaks the quantity of game & the flocks of deer were all new to us. From thence we proceeded to oxford. We were charmed with the appearance of the town. The colledges are antient & picturesque, the streets board & the land-cape rendered perfect by the lovely Isis which spreads into broad placid expanse of water & runs south of the town. we had letters to several of the professors who received us with great politeness & cordiality. we found that regulations of this university were much improved since the days of Gibbon; But there is still in fashion a great deal of bigotry & devotion to established rules constrains the mind of the students to slavish & narrow principles of action many enormities are also practised which although they might excite the laughter of a stranger were looked upon in the of the University as matters of the utmost consequence. Some of the gentlemen obstinately wore light coloured pantaloons when it was the rule of the colledge to wear dark; the masters were angry & their resolves resolute so that while on stage were there two of the students were on the point of being expelled on this very question. The threatened severity caused a considerable change in the costume of the gentlemen for several days

Such to our infinite astonishment we found to be the principal topic of conversation when we arrived in the town. our minds had been filled with the remembrance of the events that had been transacted here above a century & half before. It was here that Charles I had collected his forces; this town had been faithful to him when the whole nation had forsaken him to join the standard of parliament & liberty. It was strange to us. entered the town full of the our thoughts now occupied by the memory that unfortunate king, the amiable Fashland and the insolent Gower and but we found it filled with good townsmen & students who think of nothing else than these events. Yet there are some relics to remind you of antient times; among others we regard notebook. By April the following year she had finished her draft of *Frankenstein*, which organized the chapters into two volumes.

Except for a small number of missing pages, the manuscript of this draft has survived. The pages have long since been torn from the original notebooks and are now loose sheets. Everywhere on these sheets, alongside Mary's draft, one can see Shelley's corrections, revisions and additions. He amends awkward words and loose constructions (particularly in the early chapters), suggests word changes, and adds short passages. He appears to have corrected while Mary was composing, taking the notebook from her and revising her text chapter by chapter. Sometimes his notes catch the tone of his voice. At one point Mary writes: 'We were also shewn a room which the Lord Chancellor Bacon [i.e. Francis Bacon] had inhabited'; 'no sweet Pecksie' writes Shelley in the margin, ''twas fri<u>ar</u> Bacon the discoverer of gunpowder'. Mary duly revises her sentence to read: 'We were also shewn a room which \Frier/ Bacon \the discoverer of gunpowder/ [i.e. Roger Bacon] had inhabited.'

To take one example of Shelley's contribution to *Frankenstein*: early in the novel Frankenstein compares his character with that of his cousin Elizabeth. Mary's original draft reads:

> I was more calm and philosophical than my companion[.] Yet I was not so mild or yielding. My application was of longer endurance than hers but it was not so severe as hers whil[e] it lasted[;] my amusements were studying old books of chemistry and natural magic[,] those of Elizabeth were drawing & music.

Shelley has altered and expanded this to read:

> I was more calm and philosophical than my companion[.] Yet I was not so mild or yielding. My application was of longer endurance but it was not so severe whilst it endured. I delighted in investigating the facts relating to the actual world, she busied herself in following the aerial creations of the poets. The world was to me a secret which I desired to discover, to her it was a ~~haven~~ vacancy which she sought to people with imaginations of her own.[7]

In April Mary Shelley began to transcribe a fair copy of *Frankenstein* into perhaps eleven small, softback exercise books. This more legible text could then be taken to publishers for consideration. Only a small part of this fair copy has survived, again as loose sheets. For some unknown reason, Shelley copied out the last few pages of Mary's fair copy. He and Mary then tried to get the novel published. It was shown to Byron's publisher, John Murray, who was impressed by it ('Murray likes F.' Mary wrote in her journal on 26 May),[8] but his adviser, William Gifford, advised him not to publish it. On 3 August 1817 Shelley sent the manuscript to his own publisher, Charles Ollier, taking care not to reveal the identity of the author: 'I send you with this letter a manuscript which has been consigned to my care by a friend in whom I feel considerable interest'.[9] Ollier seems to have read the novel – 'I hope Frankenstein did not give you bad dreams', Shelley wrote to him a few days later – but declined to publish it.[10]

Finally, it was accepted by Lackington, Allen and Company, and again Shelley did not divulge that Mary was the author: 'I ought to have mentioned that the novel which I sent you is not my own production, but that of a friend who not being at present in England cannot make the correction you suggest. As to any mere inaccuracies of language I should feel myself authorized to amend them when revising proofs.'[11] *Frankenstein, or the Modern Prometheus* was published on New Year's Day 1818. (figure 34) The following day Shelley sent a copy of the book to Walter Scott. His own share, he wrote, consisted simply in having superintended the proofs through the press 'during the Author's absence'.[12] Scott's favourable review, suggesting that Shelley was the author, appeared in March. In June, Mary Shelley thanked Scott for his review of *Frankenstein*, and enlightened him as to its author:

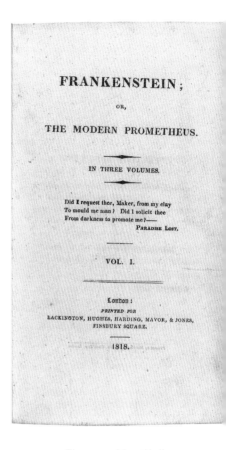

> M[r] Shelley soon after its publication took the liberty of sending you a copy but as both he and I thought in a manner which would prevent you from supposing that he was the author we were surprised therefore to see him mentioned in the notice as the probable author. – I am anxious to prevent your continuing in the mistake of supposing M[r] Shelley guilty of a juvenile attempt of mine; to which – from its being written at an early age, I abstained from putting my name – and from respect to those persons from whom I bear it. I have therefore kept it concealed except from a few friends.
>
> I beg you will pardon the intrusion of this explanation.[13]

Figure 34 Mary Shelley, first edition of *Frankenstein* (1818). Oxford, Bodleian Library, Arch. AA e.167.

'a devout but nearly silent listener'

Mary Shelley's letter to Walter Scott is striking for its diffidence: she is worried that *Frankenstein*, her first literary work, might sully the names of Godwin, Wollstonecraft and Shelley. Godwin himself, however, had no such fears. In February 1823 he wrote to his daughter in Italy assuring her that she had the talent to support herself by writing:

> Do not, I intreat you, be cast down about your worldly circumstances. You certainly contain within yourself the means of your subsistence. Your talents

are truly extraordinary. Frankenstein is universally known; &, though it can never be a book for vulgar reading, is every where respected. It is the most wonderful work to have been written at twenty years of age that I ever heard of.[14]

Later that year he arranged for a second edition of *Frankenstein*, which was published in August 1823, while Mary was still in Italy. This time, the name of the author was given: 'Mary Wollstonecraft Shelley'.

In February 1831 Henry Colburn and Richard Bentley launched a series of monthly one-volume reprints. The second of these 'Standard Novels' was Godwin's *Caleb Williams*; the fifth was *St. Leon*; the ninth, published in October 1831, was *Frankenstein*. The publishers advertised it as 'Mrs. Shelley's celebrated Romance of Frankenstein, With a new Introduction, explanatory of the origin of the Story, by the Author, and containing original Anecdotes of Lord Byron, &c.'

Frankenstein is a novel of several voices. We hear the articulate voice of the creature in his extraordinary impassioned dialogues with his creator. We hear Frankenstein's voice in the long narrative of his life he gives to Walton. Walton's own voice is heard in the letters to his sister which open and close the novel, and which describe his obsessive northward journey through the ice. The long introduction Mary Shelley wrote in 1831 added a fourth voice, which in its substance and tone joins seamlessly with the rest of the novel. Here, she vividly recalls the summer spent at Geneva: the 'incessant rain' that 'confined us for days to the house'; the volumes of ghost stories 'translated from the German into French' that fell into their hands, and Byron's proposition, 'We will each write a ghost story.' Her description of the dream that provided the germ of the novel has become famous:

> I saw – with shut eyes, but acute mental vision – I saw the pale student of unhallowed arts kneeling beside the thing he had put together. I saw the hideous phantasm of a man stretched out, and then, on the working of some powerful engine, show signs of life, and stir with an uneasy, half-vital motion. … He sleeps; but he is awakened; he opens his eyes; behold, the horrid thing stands at his bedside, opening his curtains and looking on him with yellow, watery, but speculative eyes.
>
> I opened mine eyes in terror. The idea so possessed my mind, that a thrill of fear ran through me, and I wished to exchange the ghastly image of my fancy for the realities around. I see them still; the very room, the dark *parquet*, the closed shutters, with the moonlight struggling through, and the sense I had that the glassy lake and white high Alps were beyond. …
>
> On the morrow I announced that I had *thought of a story*. I began that day with the words, 'It was on a dreary night of November,' making only a transcript of the grim terrors of my waking dream.

Mary also attempts to answer the question 'so very frequently asked me – How I, then a young girl, came to think of and to dilate upon so very hideous an idea?' It is hardly surprising, she writes, that, 'as the daughter of two persons of distinguished literary celebrity, I should very early in life have thought of writing'. She remembers how Shelley 'was from the first, very anxious that I should prove myself worthy of my parentage, and enrol myself on the page of fame'. She recalls the long, frequent conversations between Shelley and Byron, 'to which I was a devout but nearly silent listener', and how Shelley urged her to develop her initial idea: 'I certainly did not owe the suggestion of one incident, nor scarcely of one train of feeling, to my husband, and yet but for his incitement it would never have taken the form in which it was presented to the world.'

In this introduction, which has become almost as well known as the novel itself, Mary partly explains the origins and development of *Frankenstein* by reference to her literary parentage, her upbringing, and her relationship with Shelley. Since then, the surviving manuscripts have revealed in great detail the close, critical interest that Shelley took in its production. *Frankenstein* remains, nevertheless, Mary's own achievement. Her distinctive voice can still be heard underneath the revisions and biographical anecdotes, and the later, seemingly endless, interpretations and adaptations. It is possible, indeed, for the curious to approach *Frankenstein* in reverse chronological order: one might start with one of the wilder Hammer films of the 1960s, which bear hardly any relation to the novel, and then to the celebrated James Whale film of 1931, with Boris Karloff as the creature. Then one could turn to the novel itself, first in the 1831 edition, and then in the original version of 1818. And now, in the latest edition of *Frankenstein*[15], the reader can go back to the text before Shelley's revisions, to the words that the eighteen-year-old Mary Shelley first entered into a newly bought notebook one summer in Geneva.

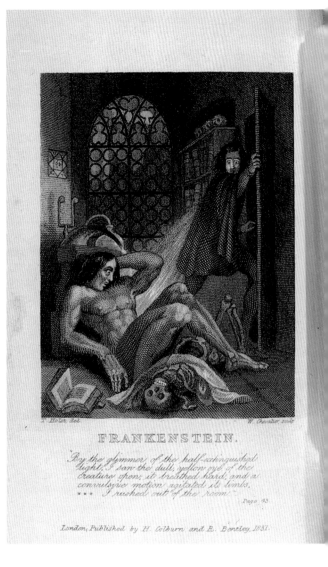

FRANKENSTEIN.

'By the glimmer of the half-extinguished light, I saw the dull, yellow eye of the creature open; it breathed hard, and a convulsive motion agitated its limbs.
*** I rushed out of the room.'
Page 43

London, Published by H. Colburn and R. Bentley, 1831.

Figure 35 Mary Shelley, third edition of *Frankenstein* (1831) with the first illustration of the Creature. Oxford, Bodleian Library, Buxton 201.

Figure 36 *pp. 90–91* E. Finden, *Diodati. The Residence of Lord Byron* (1833). Private collection.

FRANKENSTEIN.

"By the glimmer of the half-extinguished
light, I saw the dull, yellow eye of the
creature open; it breathed hard, and a
convulsive motion agitated its limbs.
*** I rushed out of the room."

Page 43.

T. Holst, del.   W. Chevalier, sculp.

The first illustration of the Creature, Frankenstein

Engraved for the third edition of Mary Shelley's
Frankenstein, 1831.

Buxton 201

Printed in UK/CP2139 Website: shop.bodleyox.ac.uk

Price : £   0.60

331198

**Shelley Composing *Prometheus Unbound*
in the Baths of Caracalla, Rome**
by Joseph Severn, 1845.
With kind permission of Lord Abinger

Printed in UK/CP2142 Website: shop.bodleyox.ac.uk

✤ 6 ✤

Shelley's Death

Dreams and visions

'My imagination, unbidden, possessed and guided me', wrote Mary of the dream that led to *Frankenstein*, 'gifting the succession of images that arose in my mind with a vividness far beyond the usual bounds of reverie.' Her memories of her last days with Shelley have something of this vividness, and in the days and months after his death her imagination, intensified by grief and solitude, formed an image of him that became, perhaps, the chief devotion of the rest of her life. This devotion was partly expressed through a painful but fruitful struggle with his manuscripts.

Shelley and Mary spent their last summer together in San Terenzo, a remote village in the Bay of Spezia. Their home, the Villa Magni, was a former boathouse. They and their surviving child, Percy Florence, shared it with their friends Edward and Jane Williams, and for a time with Claire Clairmont, so living conditions were cramped. A wooded hill rose steeply behind the house, and at high tide the sea came right to the door. Shelley delighted in the surroundings, and spent much of his time out in his boat, the *Don Juan*, drafting his final, enigmatic poem *The Triumph of Life*. (Figures 38–39) Mary detested the remoteness and sense of desolation; she hated the wretchedly poor, almost savage villagers, who spoke an impenetrable dialect and at times of festival danced all night on the sands close to their door, wailing a single tune, over and over again. At Villa Magni she had a near fatal miscarriage, and Claire was told of the death of her daughter Allegra, aged just five.

In times of extreme nervousness Shelley experienced vivid dreams and visions. In the middle of one night he rushed screaming into Mary's room. Mary, who was still unable to walk after her miscarriage, tried unsuccessfully to wake him then, panic-stricken, ran across the hall to Jane Williams's room, falling against her door. Edward Williams went to Shelley who, now awake, told him of his dream. 'What had frightened him was this', Mary later told her friend Maria Gisborne:

Figure 37 Daniel Roberts, view of the *Don Juan* and the Villa Magni. The scene in 1822, drawn from memory some years later. Eton College.

Compelling them

With several beams enwreathing the thoughtless crowd
So distinct

Thus on the wew
Mask after mask fell from the countenance
And form of every pilgrim
And from of all, ~~~ when the day
Has old the joy which was when when
Perished the shapes in the thirsin valley
not my grew weary of the ghastly dance

And sunk self, as I have fallen by the
Those sweetest, from whose brows
from those power most shadows
And coast of beauty & beauty had abide
them,
And what is life I said... the
this eye upon the distant car of beams
Onward,   so of that what most be the day

And answered.... Happy they for whom the
Of

Figure 38 *far left* P.B. Shelley, final surviving lines of *The Triumph of Life* (1822). Oxford, Bodleian Library, MS. Shelley adds. c. 4, fols 52v + 53r.

Figure 39 *left* Edward Williams, self-portrait. Oxford, Bodleian Library, [pr.] Shelley adds. e. 7.

Figure 40 *p. 96* Guitar presented by P.B. Shelley to Jane Williams. Oxford, Bodleian Library, Shelley relics 1. Photo: Nick Cistone.

Figure 41 *p. 97* Portrait of Jane Williams by George Clint. Oxford, Bodleian Library, Shelley relics 4.

He dreamt that lying as he did in bed Edward & Jane came into him, they were in the most horrible condition, their bodies lacerated – their bones starting through their skin, the faces pale yet stained with blood, they could hardly walk, but Edward was the weakest & Jane was supporting him – Edward said Get up, Shelley, the sea is flooding the house & it is all coming down. S. got up, he thought, & went to the his [*sic*] window that looked on the terrace & the sea & thought he saw the sea rushing in. Suddenly his vision changed & he saw the figure of himself strangling me, that had made him rush into my room, yet fearful of frightening me he dared not approach the bed, when my jumping out awoke him, or as he phrased it caused his vision to vanish.[1]

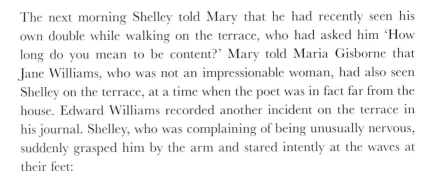

The next morning Shelley told Mary that he had recently seen his own double while walking on the terrace, who had asked him 'How long do you mean to be content?' Mary told Maria Gisborne that Jane Williams, who was not an impressionable woman, had also seen Shelley on the terrace, at a time when the poet was in fact far from the house. Edward Williams recorded another incident on the terrace in his journal. Shelley, who was complaining of being unusually nervous, suddenly grasped him by the arm and stared intently at the waves at their feet:

> Observing him sensibly affected I demanded of him if he was in pain – but he only answered, saying 'There it is again! – there!' – He recovered after some time, and declared that he saw, as plainly as he then saw me a naked child rise from the sea, clap its hands as if in joy and smiling at him. This was a trance that it required some reasoning and philosophy entirely to awaken him from, so forcibly had the vision operated on his mind. Our conversation which had been at first rather melancholy lead [sic] to this, and my confirming his sensations by confessing that I had felt the same, gave a greater activity to his ever wandering and lively imagination.[2]

In a generally light-hearted essay on ghosts, written in 1824 for the *London Magazine*,[3] Mary Shelley distinguished the ghosts of popular fiction, 'the true old-fashioned, foretelling, flitting, gliding ghost', from shadows and unreal phantoms. The former – 'The returning bride, who claims the fidelity of her betrothed; the murdered man who shakes to remorse the murderer's heart; ghosts that lift the curtains at the foot of your bed as the clock chimes one' – were purely fantastical; the latter 'appalled the senses' of those who saw them, but were considered by others to be no more than delusions or optical deceptions. For herself, she wrote, she had only seen a ghost once, in a dream, but she did remember experiencing uncanny feelings while wandering through the rooms of the house of a recently departed friend:

> methought, I heard, I felt — I know not what — but I trembled. To have seen him but for a moment, I would have knelt until the stones had been worn by the impress, so I told myself, and so I knew a moment after, but then I trembled, awe-struck and fearful. Wherefore? There is something beyond us of which we are ignorant. The sun drawing up the vaporous air makes a void, and the wind rushes in to fill it,— thus beyond our soul's ken there is an empty space; and our hopes and fears, in gentle gales or terrific whirlwinds, occupy the vacuum; and if it does no more, it bestows on the feeling heart a belief that influences do exist to watch and guard us, though they be impalpable to the coarser faculties.

It is too much to say that Mary ever looked for, let alone saw, Shelley's ghost, but his death created a sudden void. She and her infant son were alone in Italy and facing an uncertain future, and images of Shelley that were almost palpable in their intensity and immediacy rushed in to fill the empty space. In the fraught letters Mary wrote during this period, and the pages of her private journal, he becomes 'transcendent' and 'divine'.

Adonais

Shelley and Edward Williams had set sail for the Villa Magni on 8 July 1822. On 13 July Mary and Jane Williams had learned that the wreck of a small boat and a water cask had been found. On 25 July they had heard that Shelley's and Williams's bodies had been found washed ashore. Mary never forgot the dreadful suspense of those days, when they were 'thrown about by hope and fear'. The bodies were cremated on the beach on 15 and 16 August, witnessed by Byron, Leigh Hunt and another friend, Edward Trelawny, who supervised the cremations and described them to Mary. Trelawny's numerous subsequent, and increasingly unreliable descriptions gave Shelley's cremation an almost mythic status. An idealized depiction of it, with Mary present, was painted in 1889 by Louis Edouard Fournier. (Figure 43)

Shelley's ashes were buried in the non-Catholic cemetery in Rome, not far from his son William, and his fellow poet John Keats. The Shelleys had known Keats only slightly in England, but when Shelley had learned of the consumption that would soon kill him he had encouraged him to visit them in Italy. Keats's cordial and carefully composed reply was preserved among the family papers. When Shelley heard of Keats's death in Rome in February 1821, he composed one his finest works, *Adonais: An Elegy on the Death of John Keats*. In the poem Shelley tells the reader to go to Rome:

> Go thou to Rome, – at once the Paradise,
> The grave, the city, and the wilderness;
> And where its wrecks like shattered mountains rise,
> And flowering weeds, and fragrant copses dress
> The bones of Desolation's nakedness
> Pass, till the Spirit of the spot shall lead
> Thy footsteps to a slope of green access
> Where, like an infant's smile, over the dead,
> A light of laughing flowers along the grass is spread.

Shelley's association with Keats (a copy of Keats's final volume of poetry was found in his jacket pocket after his death), the proximity in Rome of his, Keats's and William's mortal remains, and, not least, the greatness

To those who cannot question well
The spirit that inhabits it:
It talks according to the wit
Of its companions, and no more
Is heard than has been felt before
By those who tempt it to betray
These secrets of an elder day. —
But, sweetly as it's answers will
Flatter hands of perfect skill,
It keeps it's highest holiest tone
For our beloved Jane alone —

—

Figure 42 *left* P.B. Shelley, fair copy of *With a Guitar, to Jane*. Oxford, Bodleian Library, MS. Shelley adds. e. 3, fol. 3r.

Figure 43 *below* Edward Williams, sketch of Byron's boat, the *Bolivar*, and Shelley's boat, the *Don Juan*. Oxford, Bodleian Library, MS. Shelley adds. c. 12, fol. 26r.

Figure 44 *p. 100–1* Louis Edouard Fournier, *The Funeral of Shelley* (1889). A fictional depiction of the cremation, showing, left to right, Trelawny, Leigh Hunt, Byron; Mary Shelley (who was not in fact present) kneels behind them. Walker Art Gallery, Liverpool © National Museums of Liverpool.

Louis-Edouard Fournier
1889

P. B. Shelley Esq.

Hampstead August 16

My dear Shelley,

I am very much gratified that you, in a foreign country, and with a mind almost over occupied, should write to me in the strain of the Letter beside me. If I do not take advantage of your invitation it will be prevented by a circumstance I have very much at heart to prophecy. There is no doubt that an english winter would put an end to me, and do so in a lingering hateful manner, therefore I must either voyage or journey to Italy as a soldier marches up to a battery. My nerves at present are the worst part of me, yet they feel soothed when I think that come what extreme may, I shall not be destined to remain in one spot long enough to take a hatred of any four particular bed-posts. I am glad you take any pleasure in my poor Poem;— which I would willingly take the trouble to unwrite, if possible, did I care so much as I have done about Reputation. I received

a copy of the Cenci, as from yourself from Hunt. There is only one part of it I am judge of; the Poetry, and dramatic effect, which by many spirits now a days is considered the mammon. A modern work it is said must have a purpose, which may be the God— an artist must serve Mammon— he must have "self concentration" selfishness perhaps. You I am sure will forgive me for sincerely remarking that you might curb your magnanimity and be more of an artist, and load every rift of your subject with ore. The thought of such discipline must fall like cold chains upon you, who perhaps never sat with your wings furld for six Months together. And is not this extraordinary talk for the writer of Endymion? whose mind was like a pack of scattered cards— I am pick'd up and sorted to a pip. My Imagination is a Monastry and I am its Monk— you must explain my metaphor to yourself. I am in expectation of Prometheus every day. Could I have my own wish for its interest effected you would have it still in manuscript— or be but now

putting an end to the second act. I remember you advising me not to publish my first-blights, on Hampstead heath— I am returning advice upon your hands. Most of the Poems in the volume I send you have been written above two years, and would never have been publish'd but from a hope of gain; so you see I am inclined enough to take your advice now. I must express once more my deep sense of your kindness, adding my sincere thanks and respects for Mrs Shelley. In the hope of soon seeing you I remain

most sincerely

John Keats

Figure 45 *far left* Letter from John Keats to Percy Bysshe Shelley, 16 August 1820. Oxford, Bodleian Library, MS. Abinger c. 66, fol. 72r.

Figure 46 *left* A page from one of Shelley's notebooks, salvaged from the wreck of the *Don Juan*. Oxford, Bodleian Library, MS. Shelley adds. e. 20, fol. 37r.

of the poetry, encouraged Mary to see *Adonais* as Shelley's own elegy.
She wrote to Maria Gisborne:

> The world will surely one day feel what it has lost when this bright child of
> song deserted her – Is not Adonais his own Elegy – & there does he truly
> depict the universal woe wh[ich] should overspread all good minds since
> he has ceased to be [their] fellow labourer in this worldly scene. How lovely
> does he [ ] paint death to be and with what heartfelt sorrow does he repeat
> that line – 'But I am chained to time & cannot thence depart'.[4]

'How long do you think I shall live?', Mary asked Maria Gisborne,
'as long as my mother? then eleven long years must intervene – I am
now on the eve of completing my five & twentieth year – how drearily
young for one so lost as I!'

68

Thy little footsteps on the sands
Of some remote & lonely shore —
The print of thine infant hands
Where they can see the worm will feed no more.

Thy look when when one remember to gaze on thee

I know not thy sweet smile
Her voice did answer as me painted —
Yet knew I not that heart was broken
From which it came — & I departed
Heeding not the words then spoken —
Misery — oh misery
This world is all too wide for thee!

The footsteps on the sands are
Thine eyes are dark — thy hands are
And she is dead — & thou art dead —
And the

Some secret woes had been mine own
And they had taught me that the good
The few

That for those who are lone & weary
The road of life is long & dreary

Some hopes were buried in my heart
Whose spectres haunted me with sadness

There was a

October 2—1822. Genoa ~~September~~ the

On the eighth of July I finished my journal. This
is a curious coincidence — The date still remains, the
fatal 8th — a monument to shew that all ended
then. And I begin again? — oh never! But several
motives induce me, when the day has gone down,
and all is silent around me, steeped in sleep, to pen,
as occasion wills, my reflexions & feelings. First, I
have now no friend. For eight years I
communicated with unlimited freedom with one whose
mind, far transcending mine, awakened & guided my
thoughts; I conversed with him; rectified my errors of
judgement, obtained new lights from him, & my
mind was satisfied. Now I am alone! oh, how
alone! The stars may behold my tears, & the
winds drink my sighs — but my thoughts are
a sealed treasure which I can confide to none.
White paper — wilt thou be my confident?

Collecting manuscripts

There are echoes of Mary Wollstonecraft on a stray leaf of paper that Shelley kept among his manuscripts.[5] On one side of the leaf he has sketched trees and written a few rough lines of verse. Some of the lines Mary Shelley later drew out and published as 'To F.G.' (Fanny Godwin):

> Her voice did quiver as we parted
> Yet, knew I not the heart was broken
> From which it came – & I departed
>   Heeding not the words then spoken –
> Misery – oh misery
>   This world is all too wide for thee!

Above this are further lines, seemingly written at a later date, which Mary Shelley published separately as 'To William Shelley':

> Thy little footsteps on the sands
>   Of a remote & lonely shore
> The twinkling of thine infant hands
>   Where now the worm will feed no more
> Thy look of mingled love & glee
>   When *one* returned to gaze on thee.

It has, however, been pointed out that the first line seems to refer to phrases used by Mary Wollstonecraft in letters to describe Fanny when she was separated from her daughter. Below this on the leaf are further lines:

> Thy footsteps on the sands are fled
>   Thine eyes are dark – thy hands are still
> And she is dead – & thou art dead –
>   And the …

And at the bottom of the page:

> Some hopes were buried in my heart
>   Whose spectres haunted me with sadness
> There was a …

On the other side of the leaf are a number of rough drawings of trees, staircases and flower pots, and a few stray lines: 'These cannot be forgotten – years/ May flow'; 'Breaks thine indissoluble sleep/ Miserable'; 'When said I so? It is not my fault – it is not to be attribut[e]d [?] to

Figure 50 Mary Shelley, beginning of the 'Journal of Sorrow', 2 October 1822. Oxford, Bodleian Library, MS. Abinger d. 30, fol. 1r.

me'. On one flowerpot Shelley has written the words: 'I drew this flower pot in October 1816 and now it is 1817'.

As so often with Shelley's manuscripts, it is difficult to trace precisely the various layers of draft, revision and later addition; to link the poetry usefully to events in Shelley's life; to find significance in the various sketches and doodles. Do the lines beginning 'Thy voice did quiver as we parted' describe Shelley's final meeting with Fanny before her suicide, an event which shook him deeply? Did he return to the lines in 1817, on the anniversary of Fanny's death, and add to them? Do the various flowerpots suggest a graveyard, or the staircases the progression from one state to another? What is clear is that Shelley has returned to one of his manuscripts after a year, and found in the palpability of its paper and ink an evocative reminder of past thoughts and feelings.

One of William Godwin's first actions, in the weeks after Mary Wollstonecraft's death, was to collect together her manuscripts. After Shelley's death Mary likewise sought out tangible remains: she asked a painter friend from their time in Rome, Amelia Curran, to send her the portrait that she had made of Shelley; she managed to obtain, from a reluctant Leigh Hunt, Shelley's heart, which Trelawny had pulled from the ashes after the flames had failed to consume it. Her attention then turned to his manuscripts. She was fortunate, she told Maria Gisborne, to have lived with 'a superior being among men, a bright planetary spirit enshrined in an earthly temple'; death would eventually put an end to her anguish, but for now she could 'conceive but of one circumstance that could afford me the semblance of content – that is the being permitted to live where I am now in the same house, in the same state, occupied alone with my child, in collecting His manuscripts – writing his life, and thus go easily to my grave'.[6]

Mary spent the winter of 1822–23 at Albaro on the outskirts of Genoa. She rose at eight, and spent the morning reading, collating and copying Shelley's manuscripts. In the afternoons she either walked or continued with her work. Byron sent on her desk, in which she discovered locks of hair belonging to Shelley and their daughter Clara, and letters dating from 1817–18, when they had lived at Marlow in Buckinghamshire: 'they are full of William – Clara & Allegra' she told Jane Williams, 'I was in another world while I read them – when I had done even my Percy seemed a dream – for they were here – warm & living as he – & I am still here but they are not.'[7] She noticed, with some annoyance but no great surprise, that Byron had read the letters before giving them to her; 'there was a lock of my S's hair & one of my Clara's'.

Mary asked Maria Gisborne for the most interesting letters that Shelley had written to her and her husband (either the originals or copies would do), and a transcript of the poem he had addressed to her. She was also aware of certain papers still in England and sent anxious and impatient requests to recover them. She did not like the idea of these papers being out of her possession and beyond her control. She knew, for instance, that on their departure for Italy they had left in Marlow a number of books and a box of their manuscripts, including two of her journals. She also knew that Shelley had sent some poems and prose to his publisher in England, Charles Ollier, including *A Defence of Poetry*. She asked their friend from England, and Shelley's executor, Thomas Love Peacock, to send her all he could. She was in a hurry to get things back, particularly when she heard that certain manuscripts might be published without her consent. 'I wish for the papers Peacock is to send out to me', she wrote to Maria Gisborne in November:

> I wish *all* Mss. to be sent without any exception & that as soon as possible. I have heard from Miss Curran, she is in Paris, & My Shelley's picture is at Rome – nothing can be done therefore with regard to that – so pray let me have the Mss. without any delay. If you shd receive a packet from Miss Kent directed to me pray send it with them. But let me entreat you, as you love me, to *wait* for nothing – but the very *moment* the Mss. are obtained from P to send them to me – sending me the bill of lading. This is of more consequence to me than you think. …
>
> I hear through Hunt's nephew that Peacock has given the 'Essay on Poetry' to be published for the Liberal & Peacock added that he had other Mss. of Shelleys – which says Young Hunt – 'We will procure' – now I am convinced there is *nothing* perfect and I will _all_ to be sent to me without delay, & nothing but this 'Essay on poetry' to be given to the Liberal. Pray let all Mss. of whatever kind – letters &c be sent to me immediately.

Other possibilities occurred to her. An early friend of Shelley's, Elizabeth Hitchener, had, she believed, some manuscripts: 'you would afford me the greatest consolation I am capable of having & d[o me an act] of *real, real* friendship if you wd stir yourselves to get them', she told Maria Gisborne. Hogg or Peacock might know where she had lived. Then there were the manuscripts that Harriet Shelley undoubtedly once owned, and which were now probably in the possession of her sister Eliza: 'I fear it would be utterly useless to endeavour to get them from her. But she being married – God knows – the thing might be tried, & the pleasure done to me immense.'[8]

'I shunned the face of man' says Frankenstein after the death of Justine; 'all sound of joy or complacency was torture to me; solitude was my only consolation – deep, dark, death-like solitude'. Mary Shelley had only two companions that winter in Albaro. The first was her son, Percy Florence. 'Solitary as I am, I feed & live on imagination only', she told Jane Williams, 'feelings are my events – sorrow, deep, deep & eternal my companion – Indeed I am so much alone that I should

LAST NIGHT
OF THE COMPANY'S PERFORMING THIS SEASON.

Theatre Royal, English Opera House, Strand.

This Evening, SATURDAY, October 4th, 1823,

Will be presented (*Fifteenth Time this Season*) the *Melo-Drama*, in Two Acts, called The

MILLER's MAID.

The OVERTURE and new MUSICK composed by Mr. JOLLY.

The Miller, Mr. BARTLEY,   George, Mr. T. P. COOKE,
Giles,   Mr. RAYNER,
Matty Marvellous,   Mr. W. BROWN,
Old Granger, Mr. ROWBOTHAM,   James, Mr. R. PHILLIPS,
Gamekeeper, Mr. SALTER,   Robert, Mr. SHERIFF.

Dame, Mrs. GROVE,
Phœbe, *(the Miller's Maid)* Miss KELLY.

After which (for the THIRTY-SEVENTH TIME) a new ROMANCE of a peculiar interest, entitled

PRESUMPTION:
OR, THE
FATE OF FRANKENSTEIN.

With new Scenes, Dresses and Decorations.——The MUSICK composed by Mr. WATSON.

Frankenstein, *(second time)* Mr. ROWBOTHAM,
De Lacey, *(a banished Gentleman)* Mr. W. BENNETT,   Felix De Lacey, *(his Son)* Mr. BROADHURST,
Fritz, Mr. KEELEY,   Clerval, Mr. J. BLAND,   William, Master BODEN,
Hammerpan, Mr. SALTER, Tanskin, Mr. SHIELD, Guide, Mr. R. PHILLIPS, Gypsey, Mr. SHERIFF,
(------) Mr. T. P. COOKE.

Elizabeth, *(Sister of Frankenstein)* Mrs. AUSTIN,   Agatha De Lacey, Miss L. DANCE,
Safie, *(an Arabian Girl)* Miss HOLDAWAY,   Madame Ninon, *(Wife of Fritz)* Mrs. J. WEIPPERT.

At the end of which, Mr. BARTLEY will deliver the

FAREWELL ADDRESS
OF THE SEASON.

To conclude with *(Thirty-seventh Time)* the MUSICAL FARCE, in Two Acts, called

GRETNA GREEN.

The MUSICK composed by Mr. REEVE.

Lord Lovewell, Mr. J. BLAND,   Mr. Tomkins, Mr. W. BENNETT,
Mr. Jenkins, Mr. WRENCH,   Larder, Mr. POWER,
Waiters, Postilions, &c. Messrs. Mears, Lodge, Smith, Tett, &c.

Emily,   Mrs. AUSTIN,
Betty Finnikin,   Miss KELLY.

Miss KELLY
will perform, This Evening, *The Miller's Maid* and *Betty Finikin.*

☞ *The unabated attraction of* PRESUMPTION: *or, the* FATE OF FRANKENSTEIN! *and the continued applications for Boxes, induce the Manager to announce, that it will be performed This Evening.*

Boxes 5s. Second Price 3s. *Pit* 3s. Second Price 1s. 6d. *Lower Gallery* 2s. Second Price 1s. *Upper Gallery* 1s. Second Price 6d.
Boxes, Places, Private and Family Boxes, may be had of Mr. STEVENSON, at the Box-Office, Strand Entrance, from 10 till 5.
Doors open at half-past Six, begins at Seven.—VIVAT REX.—No Money returned.—[Lowndes, Printer, Marquis Court, Drury Lane.

☞ THE GREAT SALOON will be opened as an Illuminated
CONSERVATORY,
for the reception of the Visitors of the Theatre at SECOND PRICE, which will commence at NINE o'clock.

forget how to converse with any but the dead & absent, were it not for my child.'[9] Her other companion was her journal, 'The Journal of Sorrow', to which she confided her innermost thoughts. Sometimes they are addressed directly to Shelley, whom she imagined 'with a clearness that mocks reality': 'Dearest Shelley! Have some compassion on me – give me some force – some hope (not of earthly but spiritual good) – raise me from self depression – fill me, my chosen one, with a part of your energy, & angelic nobility of spirit.'[10]

In March 1823 Peacock sent a box of material to Italy. It probably included manuscripts of two of Shelley's poems, *Julian and Maddalo* and *The Witch of Atlas*, and a prose work, *On the Vegetable System of Diet*; the transcript Mary had requested of Shelley's 'Letter to Maria Gisborne', and the manuscript of her second novel, *Valperga*, which was published later that year for her father's financial benefit. Peacock had not, however, been able to recover the box of material left at Marlow. When the Shelleys left England Peacock had given this box to their Marlow landlord, Richard Madocks, for safekeeping. Madocks now refused to hand it over until he had received the money the Shelleys owed him on their departure. The failure to recover these papers would return to haunt Mary Shelley in later years.

Return to England

Mary had practical reasons for copying and collecting Shelley's manuscripts. She intended to edit an edition of Shelley's unpublished writings, and write his biography. 'I shall write his life', she wrote in her journal, '& thus occupy myself in the only manner from which I can derive consolation. That will be a task that may carry some balm. What though I weep? – What though each letter costs a tear? – All is better than inaction & not forgetfulness – that never is – but an inactivity of remembrance.'[11] Fragments of this life have survived, and cover Shelley's days at Eton and Oxford. One fragment, dated 'March 25th', has the emotional intensity of Mary's journal:

> By his works he has raised himself to that well deserved height that must make him the wonder & glory of future ages. But his private life would remain unknown & many of his most excellent qualities sleep with his beloved ashes if I did not fulfil the task of recording them. His life was in every way romantic & to have been united to him & to have been the partner of his fortunes for eight years has embued my thoughts & existence with romance. it is indeed only by help of this feeling & the indulgence that I give to it that I can in any way endure the prolongation of life marked out for me in the eternal decrees.… arraying myself in the majesty of the imagination, I give other, & in very truth, truer names to the circumstances around me. I was the chosen mate of a cerlestial [*sic*] spirit – he has left me – & I am here to learn wisdom until I am fitted to join him in his native sky.[12]

Mary hoped to remain in Italy with Percy Florence, but to do this she depended upon the goodwill of Shelley's estranged father, Sir Timothy Shelley, whom she had never met. At the beginning of 1823 Byron had written to Sir Timothy urging him to support his daughter-in-law. In his reply, now in the family papers, Sir Timothy made his views, and intentions clear:

> The mind of my Son was withdrawn from me, & my immediate Family by unworthy & interested individuals when he was about nineteen, & after a while he was led into a new Society & forsook his first associates. In this new Society he forgot every feeling of Duty & Respect to me, & to Lady Shelley.
>
>   Mrs. Shelley was, I have been told, the intimate Friend of my Son in the Life time of his first Wife, & to the time of her Death, & in no small degree as I suspect estrang'd my Son's mind from his Family, & all his first duties in Life; with that transgression on my Mind, I cannot agree with your Lordship that though my Son was unfortunate, that Mrs Shelley is innocent; on the contrary I think that her Conduct was the very reverse of what it ought to have been; and I must therefore decline all interference in matters in which Mrs Shelley is interested. As to the Child I am inclined to afford

the means of a suitable Protection & care of him in this country, if he shall be plac'd with a Person I shall approve; But your Lordship will allow me to say that the means I *can* furnish will be limited as I have important duties to perform towards others which I cannot forget.[13]

Knowing that the future welfare of her son depended on his being in England, Mary Shelley left Italy in August 1823. In the years ahead she would dedicate a good part of her life to the papers, and the posthumous fame, of her family. She did this in the face of one determined opponent, a few old friends of the poet, a forger, and her own deep-seated desire for obscurity.

7

The Family Papers

A foreign country

Mary Shelley arrived in England to find herself famous. That season an adaptation of *Frankenstein* by Richard Brinsley Peake, *Presumption: or, the Fate of Frankenstein*, was all the rage at the English Opera House in London. The production lacked the intellectual range and intensity of the novel, but Mary was nevertheless amused by it and pleased that she had occasioned such a lively and successful theatrical experience. And she liked the way the creature was represented by a series of dashes on the playbill. 'But lo & behold! I found myself famous!', she wrote to Leigh Hunt out in Italy:

> Frankenstein had prodigious success as a drama & was about to be repeated for the 23rd night at the English opera house.... On Friday Aug. 29th Jane My father William & I went to the theatre to see it. Wallack looked very well as <u>F</u> – he is at the beginning full of hope & expectation – at the end of the 1st Act. the stage represents a room with a staircase leading to <u>F</u> workshop – he goes to it and you see his light at a small window, through which a frightened servant peeps, who runs off in terror when F. exclaims 'It lives!' – Presently F himself rushes in horror & trepidation from the room and while still expressing his agony & terror ———— throws down the door of the labratory, leaps the staircase & presents his unearthly & monstrous person on the stage.[1]

She noticed that everyone stayed until the performance was over.

The following day, Mary told Hunt that for her birthday she had been to see the Gisbornes with Jane Williams. It had reminded her of Italy. Then she had gone to see Charles Lamb, whom she found 'very entertaining & amiable though a little deaf'. On the strength of *Presumption*, she said, her father had published '*for my benefit*' a new edition of *Frankenstein*, which was welcome, for it was unclear to what extent Sir Timothy Shelley, 'S.T.S.', would support her financially (although a meeting with Sir Timothy's solicitor, Whitton, had given her cause for hope). But she felt out of place in London, and wished she was back in Italy. 'Why am I not there?' she asked Hunt. 'This is

quite a foreign country to me … but for my father, I should be with you next spring – but his heart & soul are set on my stay, and in this world it always seems one's duty to sacrifice one's own desires, & that claim ever appears the strongest which claims such a sacrifice.'

This early letter anticipates something of the character of Mary's future life in England. The sociability would alternate with periods of illness and seclusion. The sense of familial duty was extended not only to her father, but to Claire Clairmont, her aunt Everina Wollstonecraft, and, after Godwin's death, her stepmother. Letters in the archive testify to the continuing presence of old friends, as well as to a few intense new friendships. Financial anxieties, and the education of her son at Harrow and Cambridge, would necessitate a drawn-out correspondence with Sir Timothy Shelley's solicitors, Whitton and Gregson (Sir Timothy got to know his grandson a little, but refused ever to meet his daughter-in-law). Like her parents, Mary would earn what she could from her pen, developing her own distinctive literary voice and building up an impressive body of work, from journalism and travel writing to biography and a number of novels: *The Last Man* (1826), *The Fortunes of Perkin Warbeck* (1830), *Lodore* (1835) and *Falkner* (1837).

Figure 53 *left* Portrait inscribed on the reverse 'Mary Shelley / Richard Rothwell R.H.A. 1800–1868'. The similarity between this and Rothwell's portrait exhibited in 1840 (Figure 52), and the posthumous miniature by Easton (Figure 55), is striking. Private Collection.

Figure 54 *below left* A portrait by Lady Shelley faintly inscribed 'Mary'. Oxford, Bodleian Library, MS. Abinger c. 83, fol. 63r.

Figure 55 *p. 120* Posthumous portrait of Mary Shelley by Reginald Easton. Said to be based on a bust modelled from a cast taken after death. Oxford, Bodleian Library, Shelley relics (d).

Figure 56 Portrait of
Leigh Hunt by Benjamin
Robert Haydon (*c*.1811).
© National Portrait
Gallery, London.

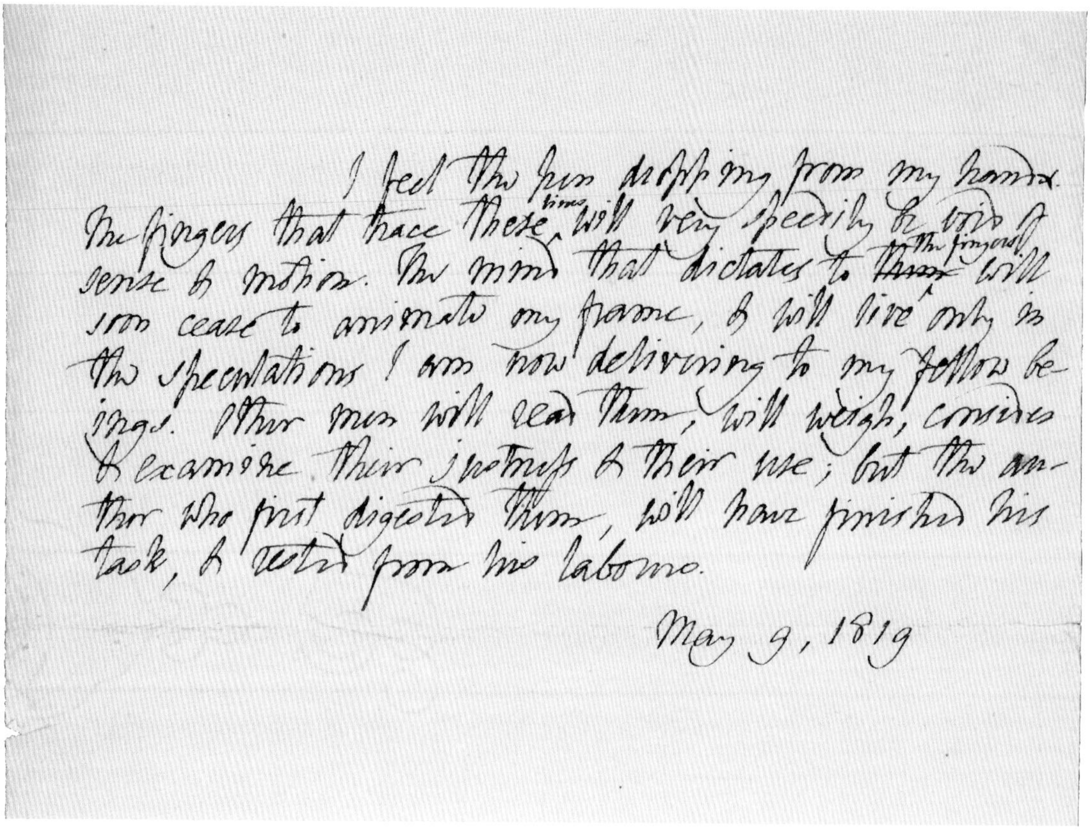

I feel the pen dropping from my hands. The fingers that trace these times will very speedily be void of sense of motion. The mind that dictates to them fingers will soon cease to animate my frame, & will live only in the speculations I am now delivering to my fellow beings. Other men will read them, will weigh, consider & examine their justness & their use; but the author who first digested them, will have finished his task, & retire from his labours.

May 9, 1819

Posthumous poems

Figure 57 Note by
William Godwin, 9 May
1819. Oxford, Bodleian
Library, MS. Abinger
c. 32, fol. 32r.

Mary Shelley's plans for an edition of Shelley's unpublished work began well. In November 1823, with the support of the poet Bryan Waller Procter, and the financial backing of two Shelley enthusiasts, Thomas Lovell Beddoes and Thomas Forbes Kelsall, she reached an agreement with Leigh Hunt's brother John Hunt to publish an edition of 500 copies. She suggested to Leigh Hunt that he write a short biographical notice – 'This, just at this moment would I think better come from you' – and asked him to send her the copies she had lent him of a few of Shelley's works: 'the Essay on Devils – Translation of Cyprian – Witch of Atlas and the Cyclops of Euripides'.[2] 'After all I spend a great deal of my time in solitude', she wrote to Hunt's wife Marianne, several days later. 'I have been hitherto fully occupied in preparing Shelley's MSS – it is now complete, & the poetry alone will make a large Volume. Will you tell Hunt that he need not send any of the MSS that he has (except the Essay on Devils & some lines addressed to himself on his arrival in Italy, if he should choose them to be inserted) as I have re-copied all the rest.'[3]

The phrase 'fully occupied in preparing Shelley's MSS' hardly does justice to the extraordinary efforts required to make sense of the poet's notebooks and loose papers. In a later letter to the publisher Edward Moxon Mary compared the work to cracking a code: 'The M.S. ... consisted of fragments of paper which in the hands of an indifferent person would never have been decyphered – the labour of putting it together was immense'.[4] Taking Shelley's fragments of paper, with their disparate texts and complex layers of revision and correction, she filled four notebooks with neatly written fair copies of his poetry and prose. Two of these notebooks are of Italian paper, and so probably date from Mary's winter in Albaro. The first[5] contains her copies of Shelley's prose works, including *Translation of Plato's Ion*, *Extracts translated from Plato's Republic*, *Speculations on Metaphysics*, *On Life*, *Speculations on Morals*, *A Philosophical View of Reform*, *On the Symposium*, *On the Athenians*, *The Coliseum* and *An Essay on Friendship*. The second notebook[6] is entitled 'Manuscripts in verse. Percy Bysshe Shelley. MWS.'; it contains 133 fair-copy poems and fragments, which Mary numbered and then indexed in the back of the book. Mary probably purchased the other two notebooks soon after arriving back in England. The first[7] includes fair copies of Shelley's prose essays *A Defence of Poetry* and *On Love*, and his translation of Plato's *Symposium*; the second[8] consists of further 'Poems and Fragments'.

These four notebooks are a testimony to Mary's assiduity and skill as an editor. Marks in other hands indicate that they were used by the printers when setting copy for the published texts. In 1798 Godwin – or the printer – had thrown away the press-copy manuscripts used for the *Posthumous Works* and *Memoir* of Mary Wollstonecraft, a common practice at the time. That Mary Shelley's notebooks have, by contrast, survived, and largely intact, is proof of her emotional attachment to them.

Posthumous Poems of Percy Bysshe Shelley was published in the summer of 1824. It included *Julian and Maddalo*, *The Witch of Atlas*, *Letter to Maria Gisborne*, *The Triumph of Life*, *Prince Athanase*, *Ode to Naples*, *Mont Blanc*, as well as fifty-nine 'Miscellaneous Poems', nine 'Fragments', five translations, and *Alastor*, which was included because the original volume, published in 1816, was now very scarce (even Mary had found it difficult to track down a copy). Leigh Hunt never wrote the biographical notice Mary had asked for, so she wrote a short introduction instead. It was her first opportunity to share publicly her recollection of the poet's character, to relate the poetry to the poet. She recalled his love of nature and solitude; his fragile health; his enthusiasm for a sacred cause, 'the improvement of the moral and physical state of mankind'; his transparent goodness and intellectual brilliance. She also explained her decision to publish his poetic fragments:

Many of the Miscellaneous Poems, written on the spur of the occasion, and never retouched, I found among his manuscript books, and have carefully copied. I have subjoined, whenever I have been able, the date of their composition.

I do not know whether the critics will reprehend the insertion of some of the most imperfect among these; but I frankly own that I have been more actuated by the fear lest any monument of his genius should escape me than the wish of presenting nothing but what was complete to the fastidious reader. I feel secure that the lovers of Shelley's poetry (who know how, more than any other poet of the present day, every line and word he wrote is instinct with peculiar beauty) will pardon and thank me: I consecrate this volume to them.

She concluded with the news that a selection of Shelley's prose works would soon be published.

'The ungrateful world did not feel his loss', wrote Mary in her preface, 'and the gap it made seemed to close as quickly over his memory as the murderous sea above his living frame.' She was determined that Shelley's name should be better known. Unfortunately, Sir Timothy Shelley was equally determined that it should not. He wished an end to the heterodox opinions and notoriety his son had attached to the family name. As soon as he learned of the *Posthumous Poems* he temporarily stopped the small allowance he had granted Mary to support her son, and demanded that the unsold copies be withdrawn. Furthermore, he sought to block the publication of the prose works by insisting that the manuscripts be given to Thomas Love Peacock. He wanted an assurance that henceforth none of Shelley's work would be published, nor his name be mentioned in print. If these demands were not met, then he would stop his allowance altogether. Mary had no choice but to agree, and consoled herself with the thought that, now aged seventy, Sir Timothy surely had only a short time left to live. In August Peacock told Whitton that he had 'received from Mrs. Shelley the *original* MSS. which were to have composed the prose volume'. There were two translations from Plato in other hands, but Mrs Shelley had assured him that they would not be published, and that they would soon be sent to him. [9]

Henceforth Mary Shelley's transmission of her knowledge of her husband was surreptitious and implicit. She helped from behind the scenes with the pirated edition of Shelley's poetry published in France by the Galignani brothers in 1829. The character of Adrian, Earl of Windsor in her novel *The Last Man* is immediately recognizable as Shelley. She also shared her manuscripts privately. In 1826 she offered to send her friend John Bowring 'some prose Mss. of Shelley's' along with some letters, 'but these would be to be read by you only'. [10] In an undated letter Mary Diana Dods thanks Mary for 'Shelleys beautiful

Letters'; 'why do you not publish them?' she asked, 'they would do more good to his memory than all that Friends can say – they contain in themselves such perfect and decided refutation of many of the silly calumnies floating abroad – it is to be *wish'd* for his sake and yours – it is *necessary* for your Son's – Plato's Banquet – but that shall be talk for us anon – it is charming.'[11]

Posthumous fame

William Godwin died in 1836, leaving a final book, *The Genius of Christianity Unveiled*, in manuscript. In his *Memoir* of Mary Wollstonecraft he had argued that 'every benefactor of mankind is more or less influenced by a liberal passion for fame', and had written of his curiosity 'to be acquainted with the scenes through which they had passed, and the incidents that had contributed to form their understandings and character'. Over the course of his long life he had carefully built up an extensive archive of correspondence and literary manuscripts in anticipation of his survivors tracing his life through his papers and thereby satisfying his own passion for fame. He had composed a number of autobiographical fragments covering his early years, and methodically maintained his journal. In a note written in 1819 he had imagined the posthumous life of his archive (Figure 57):

> I feel the pen dropping from my hands. The fingers that trace these lines will very speedily be void of sense & motion. The mind that dictates to the fingers will soon cease to animate my frame, & will live only in the speculations I am now delivering to my fellow beings. Other men will read them, will weigh, consider & examine their justness & their use; but the author who first digested them, will have finished his task, & rested from his labours.[12]

His opinions on fame had changed over the years. He had published his candid memoir of Mary Wollstonecraft secure in the belief that it could only enhance her reputation, and be an inspiration to others. Later, however, in an incomplete note left among his papers, he recalled his desire to write an account of his own life, and admitted that his feelings on the subject were not what they were. He now doubted his earlier 'infinite love of ingenuousness', and intention to be 'nearly as explicit as Rousseau in the composition of his Confessions':

> ingenuousness has not always the effect of truth. Truth, practically speaking, arises from the relative character & disposition of two persons or things, the speaker & the hearer, the words uttered, & the temper of him by whom the words are received. ... The reader no sooner peruses the little section of

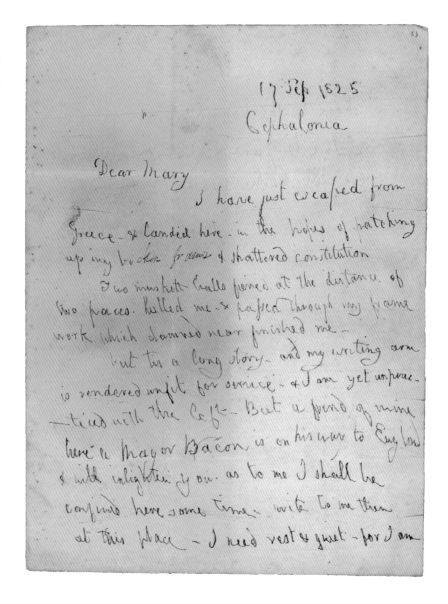

Figure 58 Letter from E.J. Trelawny to Mary Shelley, 17 September 1825, written with his left hand shortly after an attempt on his life. Oxford, Bodleian Library, MS. Abinger c. 47, fol. 53r.

narration alluded to, than he exclaims according to his own preconception, How honourable a proceeding! how arrogant a folly! how glorious a virtue! how odious a vice!

He confessed that he was 'a lover of fame, honourable fame', but wished to be judged by his writing, not his life:

I am an author. In that character the world has enough of me, upon which to fasten its misrepresentations & its criticisms. As an individual, I have never been a man of the world. I have seen a portion of human society in most of its various classes; but that is a circumstance which has arisen incidentally, & not out of any bustling & obtrusiveness of my own. I am of a retiring, not an intrusive disposition. … My personal transactions have been

too insignificant to merit the public attention, & too independent for me to
wish to expose them to the cavils of the many headed multitude.

I am an author. By my works I am content to be judged.[13]

At some point this fragment was placed inside a velvet frame. Perhaps
Lady Shelley, in her capacity as keeper of the family papers, kept it
before her as a kind of guide or credo.

In 1798 Godwin had burnt the manuscript of Mary Wollstonecraft's
comic drama because he had thought its publication would do nothing
for her reputation. A truthful literary reputation, he believed, required
some judicious destruction. In a note written two years before his death
he gave some rather vague instructions about what should be preserved
among his literary papers, and what destroyed.

With respect to these papers I know not how to decide what should be
printed, & what destroyed. Let all that are not presently printed, be
consigned to the flames. But for the consideration of profit to be made, I
should pass sentence of condemnation on nearly the whole.

The most faultless book I ever printed, is probably the Thoughts on Man.
It contains some egotism, but kept perhaps within proper bounds.

Let not a line of these papers be printed, that should stand a chance of
being justly deemed tedious or insipid.

June 30, 1834[14]

Godwin had appointed his literary daughter as his executor. So, in
addition to Shelley's papers, Mary was faced with her father's archive.
On the face of it, Godwin's manuscripts are more immediately accessible;
his writing is invariably legible and paragraphs are neatly indented; but
the sheer range and quantity of the papers – the incoming and outgoing
correspondence, the thirty-two volumes of the journal, the various
philosophical, historical and literary works, the miscellaneous fragments
– is forbidding.[15] In duty to her father, however, and to support her
widowed stepmother, Mary agreed to go through Godwin's papers with
a view to their publication. In July 1836 Mrs Godwin drew up a contract
with the publisher Henry Colburn, who agreed to pay her 350 guineas
for a two-volume edition by Mary of his memoirs and correspondence.
Mary sorted out his autobiographical fragments, and read, collated
and copied his correspondence, linking the letters with passages of
biography. Unsurprisingly, the letters and notes exchanged between her
own mother and father in 1796–97 had a special resonance:

A series of notes details the progress of their intimacy. – After her death
Godwin collected & numbered them – & with a few omissions these records
of dead passion are now before me. It is touching to see proof of how the
slightest of these notes was valued by the receiver. The writer usually

appended only the name of the day of the week – but the date of the month & year is added to all Godwin's notes in Mary Wollstonecraft's handwriting – & his own are again thus dated by Godwin. It is strange but true how the etherial all forgetful passion of love yet clings to the smallest minutia that appertains to itself – a date becomes a hallowed epoch – & while lovers would often annihilate both space & time the slightest change in these two conditions of humanity is fraught to them with the whole interest & [pleasure?] of their lives.[16]

Mary also attempted to recover some of Godwin's outgoing letters by writing requests for manuscripts to Josiah Wedgwood, William Hazlitt Jr and Henry Crabb Robinson (a friend of Coleridge and Wordsworth).

Tittle-tattle

Mary never completed her memoir of Godwin, nor did she publish the manuscript of *The Genius of Christianity Unveiled*. She not only found the process exhausting and upsetting, but feared that by publishing her father's radical and atheistical beliefs, she would draw attention to herself and her son, provoke public opinion, and so antagonize Sir Timothy Shelley. She explained to Edward Trelawny:

> With regard to my Father's life – I certainly could not answer it to my conscience to give it up – I shall therefore do it – but I must wait. I have to fight my poor Percy's battle – to try to get him sent to College without further dilapidation on his ruined prospects – & he has to enter life at College – that this should be undertaken at a moment when a cry was raised against his Mother – & that not on the question of *politics* but *religion*, would mar all – I must see him fairly launched, before I commit myself to the fury of the waves.
>
> A sense of duty towards my father, whose passion was posthumous fame makes me ready – as far as I only am concerned, to meet the misery that must be mine if I become an object of scurrility & attacks – for the rest – for my own private satisfaction all I ask is obscurity – What can I care for the parties that divide the world – or the opinions that possess it? – What has my life been – what is it Since I lost my Shelley – I have been alone – & worse – I had my father's fate for many a year a burthen pressing me to the earth – & I had Percy's education & welfare to guard over – & in all this I had no one friendly hand stretched out to support me.[17]

Despite her desire for obscurity, Mary Shelley could never – nor ever wished to – escape her literary heritage. 'As the daughter of your father & mother (known to me only by their works & opinions)', her friend the reformer Fanny Wright wrote to her in 1827, 'as the friend & companion of a man distinguished not by Genius merely but, as I imagine, by the strength of his opinions & his fearlessness in their expression – viewed only in these relations you wd be to me an object of interest'.[18] In 1837 Mary received a letter from an old friend, Harriet de Boinville, who told her that one Dr Constancio, was about to contribute 'a short Memoir of Mr Godwin to a respectable biographical publication'. He wished to obtain 'the best materials', and 'for these we naturally apply to you'. She added that they were 'looking with impatience for your own important Memoirs of Mr Godwin'.[19]

Then there were those who wished to consult her about Shelley. In 1824 Mary received an unctuous letter from Thomas Medwin, a cousin of Shelley's who had been with them for a time at Pisa. He told Mary that the death of Byron earlier that year had inspired him to write an account of their many conversations together, and that would inevitably make an appearance. Would Mary look over his text? Of course, Medwin added, if she was thinking of writing such a book herself, then he would desist at once. Mary wrote him a discouraging reply, but he persisted, and his *Conversations with Lord Byron* appeared later that year. It included, in an extended footnote, an account of Shelley's life that Mary found full of inaccuracies. 'Have you heard of Medwin's book', she asked Marianne Hunt in October, 'notes on conversations that he had at Pisa with L.B. (when tipsy) Every one is to be in it & every one will be angry he wanted me to have [a] hand in it but I declined – Years ago "When a man died the worms ate him.["] – Now a new set of worms feed on the carcase of the scandal that he leaves behind him & grow fat upon the world's love of tittle tattle – I will not be numbered among them.'[20] 'Medwin requested me to correct his MS.', she told Byron's friend John Cam Hobhouse. 'I declined even seeing it – He afterwards sent me his Memoir of Shelley – I found it one mass of mistakes – I returned it uncorrected – earnestly entreating him not to publish it – as it would be highly injurious to my interests to recall in this garbled manner past facts at a time that I was endeavouring to bring Sir T.S. to reason.'[21]

In 1829 Mary heard from Edward Trelawny. She had liked this buccaneering figure in Italy – he reminded her of a Moorish pirate – and she remained deeply grateful to him for the support he had given her in the days after Shelley's death. Since then Trelawny had corresponded with her regularly. In 1825, while fighting in Greece, he had been seriously wounded in an assassination attempt, but had still managed to write Mary a letter with his left hand. He now wrote to tell her that he was writing an account of his adventurous life, and a tribute to 'my great Love for the memory of Shelley his life & moral character'. He wanted her help: 'will you give documents – will you write anecdotes?'[22] He would, he assured her, show her the manuscript before publication. To which Mary replied:

Figure 59 Shelley composing *Prometheus Unbound* in the Baths of Caracalla, Rome, by Joseph Severn (1845). Lord Abinger.

Could you write my husband's life, without naming me it were something – but even then I should be terrified at the rouzing the slumbering voice of the public – each critique, each mention of your work, might drag me forward – Nor indeed is it possible to write Shelley's life in that way … Shelley's life must be written – I hope one day to do it myself, but it must not be published now – There are too many concerned to speak against him – it is still too sore a subject – Your tribute of praise, in a way that cannot do harm, can be introduced into your own life – But remember, I pray for omission – for it is not that you will not be too kind too eager to do me more than justice – But I only seek to be forgotten – [23]

Trelawny never acknowledged this letter, so she wrote again, adding a further reason to put him off: 'With regard to the letters it seems that an unfortunate mistake caused those I had preserved previous to our visiting Italy to be destroyed – The others are almost entirely descriptive and I mean to publish them together with the rest of his prose works at a future day'.[24] Trelawny considered this 'most unsatisfactory',[25] but Mary was adamant:

You talk of writing Shelley's life and asking me for materials – Shelley's life as far as the public had to do with it consisted of very few events and these are publickly know[n] – The private events were sad and tragical – How would you relate them, as Hunt has, slurring over the real truth – wherefore write fiction? and the truth – any part of it – is hardly for the rude cold world to handle … I have made it my earnest request to all who have meddled with our Shelley to leave me out – they have assented and I consider myself fortunate'.[26]

The family archive

Between 1834 and 1838 Mary Shelley negotiated with Edward Moxon over the complete edition of Shelley's works she had first envisaged in the months after his death. In December 1838 she agreed to sell the copyright of Shelley's writings to Moxon for £600, and to edit the poems. Old Sir Timothy Shelley, now approaching ninety, finally agreed to lift his ban on the poetry, but not on the life. *The Poetical Works of Percy Bysshe Shelley* was published in four volumes in 1839. A one-volume edition was published later that year along with Mary's edition, in two volumes, of Shelley's prose, *Essays, Letters from Abroad, Translations and Fragments* (with an 1840 title page).

The mental effort required for these monumental editions was immense. Mary spared neither herself nor the printers in achieving her desire for complete and accurate texts. 'I am afraid I gave the printer some trouble about the poems', she admitted to Moxon, 'but was earnest to have this edition complete & you cannot imagine how

Figure 60 Sir Percy
Florence Shelley. Oxford,
Bodleian Library, MS.
Photogr. c. 185 (fol. 75).

confusing & tantalizing is the turning over Manuscript books – full
of scraps of finished or unfinished poems – half illegible.'[27] The work
was done under the baleful eye of Sir Timothy Shelley, and in spite of
Mary's fear of notoriety and personal publicity. To the displeasure of
several of Shelley's friends, she felt bound to work within the prejudices
of the time and omit the anti-religious later cantos of Shelley's early
poem *Queen Mab*, and two of his most overtly radical poems, *Swellfoot
the Tyrant* and *Peter Bell the Third*. On top of this, the memories re-
awakened by the work caused her acute emotional strain. She had
circumvented Sir Timothy's ban on a life by introducing each major
poem with an extended biographical note. The intensity with which she
relives moments in her past, particularly the months before and after
Shelley's death, is compelling.

Mary Shelley had succeeded in preserving the texts of Shelley's poems, prose works and letters, and in presenting them, in print, to an increasingly receptive public. In so doing, she had preserved and enhanced the family archive. She had refused to part with any of the papers in her keeping, and, in the course of her work on Shelley and Godwin, copied a good deal of them and put them into some kind of order. She had recovered, inter alia, the stray literary manuscripts that Shelley had sent to his publisher; the long descriptive letters Shelley had sent Thomas Love Peacock from Italy; Shelley's letters to Horace Smith and Maria Gisborne; and the papers of her aunt, Everina Wollstonecraft.

Mary's wish to augment the archives with suitable acquisitions put her, briefly, into the unscrupulous hands of a notorious forger, the self-styled Major George Gordon de Luna Byron, who claimed to be the poet's son. Major Byron had got hold of some Shelley letters, probably from the box left in Marlow which Mary had failed to recover, and used them as the basis for the forgeries he put up for sale. Motivated, as she put it, by a 'desire to possess every scrap in Shelley's hand', and by a fear that the letters might be published, Mary purchased several of Major Byron's letters before finally dismissing him as an opportunistic rascal.

Mary Shelley's great solace in the last years of life was the marriage in 1848 of her son Percy Florence to Jane St John, née Gibson, a 28-year-old widow. Sir Timothy Shelley had died four years earlier, aged ninety-one, and on his death Percy Florence inherited the baronetcy and the family home, Field Place. Sir Percy Florence and latterly Jane, Lady Shelley, looked after Mary Shelley until her death in 1851, aged fifty-three. Lady Shelley, who had been devoted to Mary, saw herself as the guardian of her memory, and by extension the protective keeper of the great family archive that she and Sir Percy had inherited.

Figure 61 *left* Jane, Lady Shelley. Oxford, Bodleian Library, 2795 f.38

Figure 62 *below* Mary Shelley's travelling dressing case, with its mirror. Private collection. Photo: Nick Cistone.

Figure 63 *right* Locks of hair belonging to Shelley, William Shelley and Byron, and a bracelet fashioned from Mary Shelley's hair, kept in Mary's dressing case. Private collection. Photo: Nick Cistone.

Figure 64 *below right* A mourning ring commemorating Mary Wollstonecraft's grandfather Edward, and passed down to Mary Shelley and Lady Shelley. Kept in Mary's dressing case. Private collection. Photo: Nick Cistone.

8

The Shelley Sanctum

Precious relics

Late in life Lady Shelley recalled Mary Shelley's final moments: 'She turned her beautiful great grey eyes on us and towards her desk so often with a longing and beseeching look in them as if she wanted to speak and tell us something.' A year later, she and Sir Percy opened the desk, and for the first time learned its contents. 'There we found the private journal kept by her and Shelley from 1814, together with other precious relics.' There was also a copy of *Adonais*, with one of the pages torn loose and folded into four. 'We opened it reverently and found ashes – dust – and we then knew what Mary had so longed to tell us: all that was left of Shelley's heart lay there.'[1]

Mary Shelley left her daughter-in-law a wooden dressing case. It has remained in the family's possession, and still contains in its various compartments and pockets a number of relics, including a folding knife-and-fork set (in an original box marked 'M.W.S.'); a bracelet and a fob chain formed from Mary Shelley's hair, gathered at her death; a similar bracelet formed from the hair of Lady Shelley's first husband, Charles Robert St John, gathered when he was six years old; and locks of hair belonging to Shelley and William Shelley, contained in small packets of folded paper inscribed with lines from Petrarch by Mary Shelley. There is also an amethyst mourning ring commemorating Mary Wollstonecraft's grandfather, Edward, that had passed down to Mary Shelley and Lady Shelley. 'Her invariable jewels were Mary Wollstonecraft's amethyst ring and a diamond keeper', remembered Lady Shelley's granddaughter, 'and on her little finger a cameo ring that had belonged to the poet Shelley, which she valued more than all her possessions.'[2]

The dressing case has a fitted pocket of red leather containing an old mirror, which must once have reflected Mary Shelley's features. Lady Shelley often felt the presence of departed spirits, and indeed kept in touch. 'When I am sitting quiet I am sometimes conscious of a heavy feeling, a kind of stupor', she told Maud Brooke. 'I take my pen and then my hand seems led over the paper. I do not know what I do, but I often draw, and then between the drawings afterwards I see a name. Often it is the name of someone close to me.'[3] A quire of paper in the archive appears to contain examples of Lady Shelley's automatic writing, which record messages from her first husband and from Mary Shelley: 'Dear Love Never pray me to come to you but I charitably wait for our meeting and have an earnest and lively faith in Redeeming Goodness my own girl may you be guarded MWS.'[4] One summer she visited San Terenzo with Sir Percy, and stayed overnight in Shelley's old room in the Villa Magni: 'I spent the whole night on or near the balcony, waiting and hoping that Shelley would come to me in a vision, but alas! he did not come. I saw no vision, and Percy would not allow me to stay another night there, as he said I got no sleep. That indeed was true. How could I sleep?' While they were there Lady Shelley met an old sailor who told her of his great love for the poet: 'I pointed to my husband', she later recalled, 'who was walking round the rock near the house, and said, "There is his son." He rushed to him, threw himself down and kissed my husband's feet. "Oh, how I loved him!" he said. "He was fair, he was beautiful, he was like Jesus Christ. I carried him in my arms through the water – yes, he was like Jesus Christ." "Come and see us in our yacht," I said; "it is lying there, and we will show you some precious things."'[5]

If this incident really did take place as Lady Shelley remembered, then Sir Percy was probably acutely embarrassed. His mother had described him as 'the most guileless, unworldly & generous of human beings';[6] he was orthodox, placid and slightly overweight; he honoured the memory of 'me old father' but certainly did not worship him; he did not read much poetry, nor did he have visions. His great interests in life were yachting, bicycling and tricycling, photography, and amateur dramatics. Around the time of his mother's death he and Lady Shelley had moved to Boscombe Manor near Bournemouth. There he put on numerous amateur productions, and would eventually build a full-sized private theatre. He wrote the plays, painted the backdrops and performed some of the smaller parts.

Lady Shelley occasionally appeared in her husband's plays, but her great creation at Boscombe Manor was the Shelley Sanctum, where the precious Shelley relics were displayed, lit by a red lamp. Only members of the family and favoured guests were allowed here. Her granddaughter later described it:

Figure 65 'The Poet's Son', a portrait of Sir Percy Shelley by 'Ape' published in *Vanity Fair*. Private collection.

Figure 66 Theatrical
cartoons, possibly by Sir
Percy Florence Shelley.
Oxford, Bodleian Library,
MS. Abinger c. 83, fols 46r
and 48r.

In the boudoir was a recess known as the Sanctum, whereof the ceiling was painted with stars, under which we children talked in awed whispers, partly I think, because of the night effect, but chiefly on account of the Shelley relics that lay there, whereby as small children we became familiar with the mysterious power of things dead hands have handled. There were two cases containing Shelley MSS. bound in green volumes. The tops of these cases were of glass and covered with Roman satin of a peculiar apricot hue which reminds me quite discrepantly of nectarines. Beneath the covers lay the relics – the miniature of Shelley by the Duc de Montpensier, the Sophocles in his hand when he was drowned, bracelets of Mary Wollstonecraft's hair, and a miniature of fair little 'Willmouse' [William Shelley], who died, besides many other things, all very real and familiar to us as far back as I can remember. On the wall hung a case containing locks of hair of the poet and various of his friends and contemporaries. On the mantelpiece were some Etruscan and Greek figures and tear-bottles, and over them hung the picture of Mary Shelley now in the National Portrait Gallery.... In the Sanctum also hung Miss Curran's picture of the poet, an unfinished portrait of no great merit as a painting; but of unique interest as being the only authentic portrait of the poet except the Duc de Montpensier's pencilled drawing.

Another visitor remembered an urn in which, Lady Shelley whispered, was kept the remains of Shelley's heart. At the end of the sanctum stood a replica of the memorial Lady Shelley had commissioned from Henry Weekes, and installed in Christchurch Priory. It is a *pietà*, showing Mary cradling the drowned Shelley in her arms.

TO THE MEMORY OF
PERCY BYSSHE SHELLEY,
POET,
BORN AT FIELD PLACE IN THE COUNTY OF SUSSEX, AUGUST 4. 1792.
DROWNED BY THE UPSETTING OF HIS BOAT IN THE GULF OF SPEZZIA JULY 1822:
HIS ASHES ARE INTERRED IN THE PROTESTANT BURIAL GROUND AT ROME.

ALSO TO THE MEMORY OF
MARY WOLLSTONECRAFT SHELLEY, HIS WIFE,
BORN AUGUST 30. 1797. DIED FEBRUARY 1. 1851,
HER REMAINS ARE INTERRED. TOGETHER WITH THOSE OF HER FATHER WILLIAM GODWIN,
AND HER MOTHER MARY WOLLSTONECRAFT GODWIN,
IN THE CHURCHYARD AT BOURNEMOUTH.

"HE HAS OUT-SOARED THE SHADOW OF OUR NIGHT;
ENVY AND CALUMNY, AND HATE AND PAIN,
AND THAT UNREST WHICH MEN MISCALL DELIGHT,
CAN TOUCH HIM NOT AND TORTURE NOT AGAIN;
FROM THE CONTAGION OF THE WORLD'S SLOW STAIN
HE IS SECURE, AND NOW CAN NEVER MOURN
A HEART GROWN COLD, A HEAD GROWN GREY IN VAIN;
NOR WHEN THE SPIRIT'S SELF HAS CEASED TO BURN,
WITH SPARKLESS ASHES LOAD AN UNLAMENTED URN."

SHELLEY'S. ADONAIS.

Precious papers

As the keeper of the archive, Lady Shelley saw it as her duty to celebrate and protect the sacred memory of her family, not to serve the interests of literary scholars and biographers. But those interests would not go away, and always threatened to disturb the private, unearthly atmosphere of her Sanctum. Even worse, as far as she was concerned their ill-informed opinions contradicted the evidence of the manuscripts so carefully housed in her green leather boxes.

Lady Shelley's view of Shelley's life was simple. She exonerated the poet of all his supposed crimes, and downplayed his atheism and radical politics. In particular, she insisted that Shelley and Harriet had separated by mutual agreement before the poet met Mary. The family papers proved it. But the first attempt by Sir Percy and Lady Shelley to promote this view by sharing the archive was unsuccessful. In 1857 they asked Shelley's friend from his Oxford days, Thomas Jefferson Hogg, to write a biography. Hogg, now a lawyer, and married to Jane Williams, agreed. In March he acknowledged the arrival of the first 'box of precious papers', and thereafter sent Lady Shelley ('Wrennie') regular progress reports on *'our* book', together with assurances of his critical rigour.[7] The papers, he said, should be allowed to speak for themselves: 'To falsify documents wo^{d} be to injure the faith of history, & to destroy the credit of our book.' The *'whole* Truth' would be told,

Figure 68 *left* Henry Weekes, the Shelley Memorial at Priory Church, Christchurch, Dorset. © Helen Drinkwater.

Figure 69 *below* Portrait by Reginald Easton of T.J. Hogg playing chess at Boscombe Manor, *c.* 1857. Oxford, Bodleian Library, MS. Abinger c. 83, fol. 42r.

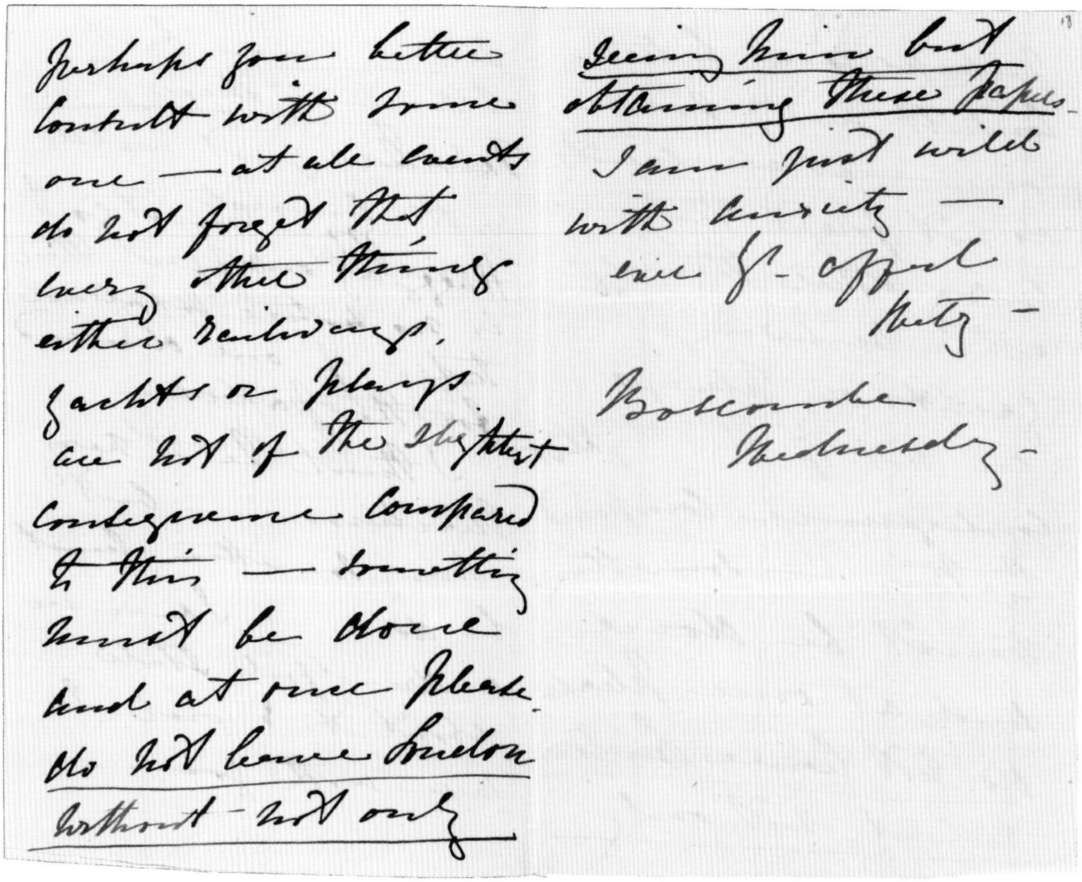

Figure 70 Letter from Lady Shelley to Sir Percy Shelley, 1857–58. Oxford, Bodleian Library, MS. Abinger c. 83, fols 17v–18r.

and he poured scorn on Trelawny, whom he knew to be writing his recollections ('A Brigand's view of the Poetic Character & Temperament is surely a monster of modern times'), and on Medwin ('I do not like these Eavesdropping *Medwins*: one is never *safe* with them'). He would be entertaining, but tactful: 'We are quite agreed, that *Our* Book *must* be *amusing*. I shall *name* as few persons, as possible, scarcely any body indeed, except the members of his own family, in the *first* edition; if it shall appear, that people are content with the manner, in wch they have been treated, it will be easy to supply the names in a subsequent edition.'

Hogg's letters to Lady Shelley are friendly but patronizing; he has a curious and rather arrogant sense of humour, and he never reveals to her what '*our* book' actually says. Reading them one can understand why Mary Shelley once called Hogg 'queer, stingy and supercilious'.[8] Whether Lady Shelley was reassured or unsettled by the letters we do not know, but when the first part of Hogg's biography was published in 1858 (in two of a projected four volumes) she was appalled by what she read. Hogg portrays 'poor Shelley' as a harmless eccentric and 'preeminently a ladies' man'; he consistently overplays his own importance in the poet's life, and freely adapts the wording of letters to suit his purpose. Lady Shelley promptly asked for the return of the boxes of papers she had given him. When Hogg replied that he had sent 'the purple box' but was retaining the others, she called her husband away from his hobbies:

Figure 71 Horoscope for P.B. Shelley. Oxford, Bodleian Library, MS. Abinger c. 82, fol. 82r.

> You must go to Hogg at once. – There is no notice whatever of our demand for the papers.
>
> I think he is very treacherous – but surely something must be done – I am in a dreadful state about it & wish I were with you – perhaps you[d] better contract with some one – at all events do not forget that every other thing either railways, yachts or plays are not of the slightest consequence compared to this – something must be done and at once[.] Please *do not leave London without not only seeing him but obtaining these papers.*
>
> I am just wild with anxiety.[9]

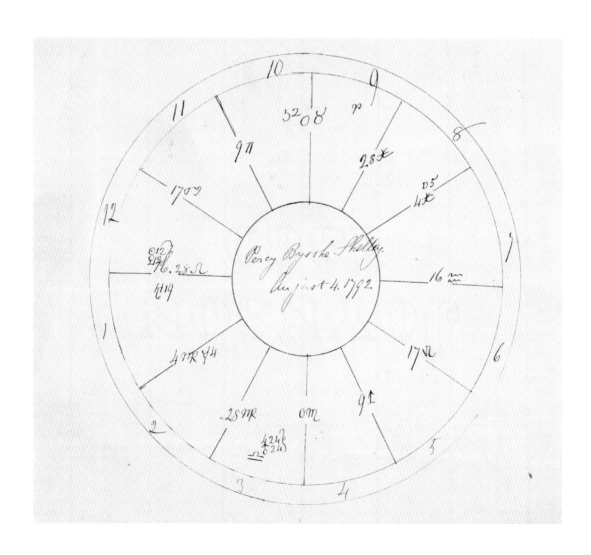

'You *must* now be well aware that my feelings as well as those of my father's sisters have been much hurt by the indiscreet use which we consider you to have made of the materials with which we provided you', Sir Percy told Hogg in May. He asked that he and Lady Shelley be shown the proofs of the second part of the biography, on the understanding they had the right to erase (before publication) any passages which 'in my opinion may tend to throw discredit and ridicule on the memories of my father & mother'.[10] When Hogg refused, Sir Percy's lawyer wrote to him promising legal action if he included any of the family's letters in subsequent volumes of his biography. These volumes were never published, and the manuscript – if it ever existed – has never been found.

Lady Shelley lacked Mary Shelley's literary knowledge and experience, and her editorial expertise. She was also, as she herself recognized, highly strung and excitable. So in 1859 she asked a 24-year-old librarian at the British Museum, Richard Garnett, to act as her friend and adviser on all matters relating to the archive. Garnett had recently published a poem in memory of Shelley; flattered, perhaps, by his immediate entry into the Shelley Sanctum, he was a loyal, sometimes uncritical advocate of Lady Shelley's view of the poet. He was also a convinced believer in astrology, and may have constructed the horoscopes of Shelley, Mary Shelley and Sir Percy Shelley that have survived in the archive.

Garnett helped in the publication, later in 1859, of *Shelley Memorials: From Authentic Sources*, edited by Lady Shelley, in which, for the first time, carefully edited versions of selected Shelley letters and journals are arranged chronologically and presented as evidence. Concerning the vexed question of Shelley's treatment of Harriet, Lady Shelley writes:

> Of those remaining who were intimate with Shelley at this time, each has given us a different version of this sad event, colored by his own views and personal feelings. Evidently Shelley confided to none of these friends. We, who bear his name, and are of his family, have in our possession papers written by his own hand, which in after years may make the story of his life complete, and which few now living, except Shelley's own children, have ever perused.[11]

In other words, Shelley's friends could not provide impartial information. Only she, as the owner of the papers, papers as yet unseen by anyone outside the family, could do that.

Old friends and new enemies

Early in 1857 Lady Shelley had invited Thomas Jefferson Hogg, Thomas Love Peacock and Edward Trelawny to Boscombe Manor. Regrettably this conference never took place. 'To assemble together under your roof three of the Poets old friends to tell their storeys [*sic*] is a pleasant dream', Trelawny replied, but he said that he 'was too old and selfish' to leave his den in Wales. As for the other two, 'indolence and excessive sensitiveness to public opinion will prevent it'.[12]

Eventually all three of these old friends of the poet fell out of favour at Boscombe. In 1858 Hogg disgraced himself with his life of Shelley. Shortly afterwards Peacock did the same. In June that year he published in *Fraser's Magazine* an account of Shelley's life, stopping shortly before the poet's separation from Harriet. He promised, in a second part,

Figure 73 Portrait of Thomas Love Peacock by Henry Wallis (1858). © National Portrait Gallery, London.

Figure 74 An example of Lady Shelley's automatic writing, dated 29 May. Oxford, Bodleian Library, MS. Abinger c. 83, fols 54r.

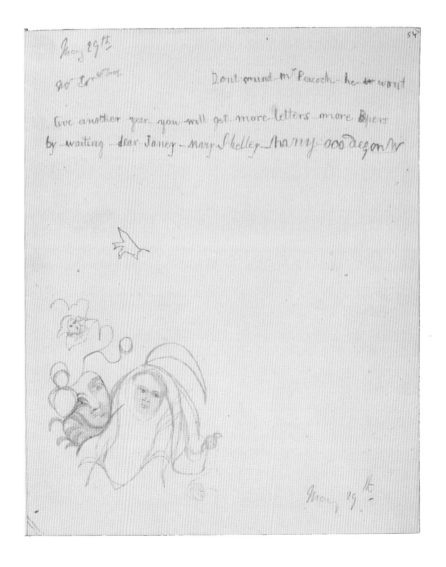

'the details of the circumstances which preceded Shelley's separation from his first wife, and those of the separation itself'.[13] He delayed publishing this second instalment until January 1860, assuming that with the publication of the *Shelley Memorials* he now had all the 'external materials' he was likely to get. But he was not satisfied with Lady Shelley's assertion that the poet had eloped with Mary after he and Harriet had agreed to separate: 'whatever degree of confidence Shelley may have placed in his several friends, there are some facts which speak for themselves and admit of no misunderstanding.… The separation did not take place by mutual consent.'[14] So far as Lady Shelley was concerned this put Peacock beyond the pale. Richard Garnett attacked him in his 1862 publication *Relics of Shelley*, while Lady Shelley was consoled by Mary's spirit: 'Don't mind Mr Peacock he wont live another year you will get more letters more Papers by waiting dear Janey – Mary Shelley.'[15]

Trelawny's memoir of Shelley, *Recollections of the Last Days of Shelley and Byron*, also appeared in 1858. This was confined to the poet's life in Italy – much safer ground – and was complimentary about Mary Shelley. Trelawny's place in the Shelley Sanctum (in the form of a portrait and a lock of his hair) was, for the moment, secure. Fourteen years later, the old adventurer was in London contemplating further reminiscences of Shelley and talking about the poet to anyone who would listen. In January 1872 he talked to William Michael Rossetti for nine hours without a break. He was also in correspondence with Claire Clairmont, who had supplied him, Richard Garnett told Lady Shelley in February, with copies of letters from Mrs Godwin to Lady Mountcashell containing 'a mass of the most malignant scandal': that Shelley had made love first to Mrs Boinville's daughter, and then to Fanny Imlay, before falling in love with Mary; that Fanny had committed suicide for his sake, and that Mrs Godwin had forced him to marry Mary because of this. But, Garnett reassured Lady Shelley, she had all the documents she needed 'for a most crushing answer':

> You have Shelley's letter to Mary immediately after Harriet's death, in which he says that he has informed his lawyer that he is 'under contract of marriage' to her (Mary), and expresses his delight at the prospect of recovering his children by this means. You have her answer, treating the marriage as a thing of course, and expressing her deep sorrow that Fanny is no longer living that she might receive her into her house, and rescue her from Mrs Godwin. You have Fanny's own letters within a few months of her death, the last only six days previously, the tone of which alone is enough to show the utter absurdity of the accusation. As to the Boinville story, you have Mrs B's letter to Mrs Shelley after Shelley's death; besides a number of minor proofs. The best of it is, however, that Mrs Godwin (for I consider that Miss Clairmont merely copies her) has

indulged in a number of palpable lies, which are easily exposed from Shelley's and Godwin's diaries, and other sources. She says that Shelley paid his addresses to Mrs Boinville's daughter early in 1814, 'they were indignant, and broke off acquaintance.' But the letter of April 18 (Hogg II, 533) shows that there was no estrangement up to that date. She says that he made love to Fanny in April of that year. That invaluable record, Godwin's diary, proves that *he never was at Godwin's at all* during that month. Better still, he did not come to town till May 18, and on May 23 Fanny departed for Wales![16]

Garnett encouraged Lady Shelley to look to the family archive, to the evidence. In 1878 Trelawny published *Records of Shelley, Byron and the Author*, in which, for reasons of his own, he now presented Mary Shelley in the most disparaging light. This, and a subsequent letter by Trelawny in *The Athenaeum* (in which, among other things, he poked mild fun at the spiritual practices that went on at Boscombe), sent Lady Shelley back to the papers. In September 1878 Sir Percy informed Garnett that, 'while I was away in the yacht', she had been 'reading all Trelawney's, Claire's & Hogg's letters &c which we possess – and she considers that with respect to showing what my mother's character was – and the estimation she was held in by all these people these papers are of great importance'.[17] It is easy to laugh at some of Lady Shelley's actions, and deplore others, but this image of her ploughing through piles of correspondence while her husband was off sailing suggests that they were motivated as much by her anxious devotion to Mary Shelley as anything else. The previous month she had written Trelawny a long, sad letter, several copies of which are in the archive:[18]

> At Boscombe, there is a room built expressly to receive all that we hold most sacred. One side is occupied by a niche in which is placed the life sized model of the monument raised to the memory of Shelley & Mary by their son …
>
> This same room is never entered but by kindred feet, or by those in whose hearts Shelley lives – Amongst other things in it, there is a glass case containing locks of hair – They belong to those he and Mary valued as friends & with whom they had been most closely associated –
>
> Leigh Hunt – Byron – Ed^d Williams & one marked – '*Trelawny 1822*' it is black, as yet, & was given, no doubt, at the time when Mary possessed in the giver a true & generous friend – But the Trelawny of those days, where is he? – Alas! that the snows of age should not only have fallen on his head but should have frozen the heart that beat so warmly in 1822 –
>
> There is a picture too, – the only one allowed to hang in the same room with those so sacred to us – again, '*Edward Trelawney*'. – These objects have been cherished under the roof of Shelley's & Mary's son, but the time has come when we must ask you whether they have any right to retain their place – and at *your bidding* they shall be removed & therefore I beg that you will answer as to this matter –

Figure 75 Copy of *Shelley and Mary* presented to the Bodleian by Lady Shelley in 1893. The label around the spine specifies the restricted access. Oxford, Bodleian Library, [pr.] Shelley e. 5.

The lock of Trelawny's hair, still black, and mounted in gilt alongside locks once belonging to Byron, Hunt, Teresa Guiccioli, Alexander Mavrocordato, Edward Williams and Thomas Moore, stayed in the family archive. The portrait, it seems, was removed from the Sanctum and hung on the landing.

Lady Shelley's trouble with Trelawny, together with the realization that neither she nor Sir Percy was getting any younger, prompted her to put the Shelley papers into an appropriate order. In 1876 a substantial number of Godwin's papers, including long extracts from his correspondence, had been published in Charles Kegan Paul's two-volume *William Godwin: His Friends and Contemporaries*. Lady Shelley now considered doing something similar with Shelley and Mary: 'the fact is', she told Garnett at the end of 1878, 'that the time has certainly arrived when all the materials we possess touching on the life of Shelley & Mary must be so arranged that at our death or before it a true statement of facts may be ready to correct the misrepresentations & misstatements which are constantly being made either by ignorant or malicious people'.[19]

The result was *Shelley and Mary*, a compilation of the Shelleys' letters and journals arranged chronologically with a few linking passages. Completed in 1882, it was very much a private production: it was printed on handmade paper, and (allegedly) just twelve copies were bound into either three or four volumes. In each copy Lady Shelley added, in pen, a few explanatory notes. She also inserted into the front of the first volume a handwritten account of 'Shelley's separation from his wife'. 'These Volumes', wrote Sir Percy in a preface, 'containing 1234 pages, have been prepared for the press by Lady Shelley, with the object of preserving from destruction the precious records in her possession. They contain all the letters and other documents of a biographical character at present in the hands of Shelley's representatives.'

Sir Percy added that *Shelley and Mary* should not be considered final, as 'it is probable that even the present extensive collection may receive additions that will ultimately render it complete'. He

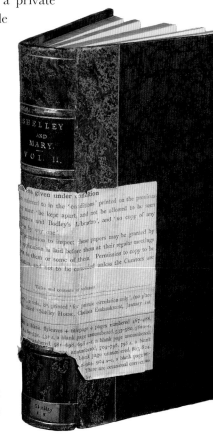

and Lady Shelley had, in fact, been augmenting the archive for some time. In 1878, for example, they had purchased a group of papers once belonging to John and Maria Gisborne, and which had passed to the Gisbornes' servant, Elizabeth Rumble, a shrewd and rather fierce old lady who had insisted that the Shelleys bid for them, along with anyone else interested, in the saleroom. They joined the Shelley letters that Mary Shelley had acquired from Maria Gisborne in the late 1830s. Richard Garnett advised Sir Percy and Lady Shelley in their acquisitions, and helped protect them from the forgeries to which Mary Shelley had once fallen victim. Major Byron had struck again in 1852, when a group of Shelley letters, published by Moxon and introduced by Robert Browning, turned out to be his forgeries. Old family feelings sometimes influenced the Shelleys' purchases. A draft letter from Sir Percy in the archive reads as follows:

> I have received a note from Mr R¹. Browning who forwards me a letter from you to him – in which you mention that Miss Clairmont wishes to sell me certain letters and papers.
>
> If these documents are of any importance they should have been given to my mother when she was engaged in publishing my father's letters in [space left in MS].
>
> I heard at the time that Miss Clairmont gave everything of any biographical or literary value to my mother for the purposes of publication.
>
> You are right in supposing that the relations between Miss Clairmont and myself are not those of intimacy. Since nearly 25 years ago by reason of circumstances which I will not trouble you with detailing I have not seen Miss Clairmont – though as in the present instance she has twice endeavoured to communicate with me through the medium of a third person.
>
> Miss Clairmont is no relation of mine. She is the daughter of *Mr & Mrs Clairmont* which last on the death of her husband became the wife of William Godwin.
>
> In answer to your application therefore I have simply to say that I decline to purchase these documents – & I may add that I feel the less disposed to make a move in the matter inasmuch as Miss Clairmont being a stranger in the Shelley family received £12000 from the money raised upon the Shelley estates. I have no right or wish of course to grudge the payment of this legacy – but I think the sum above named ought to have satisfied the lady.[20]

Biographies and bequests

The all-important Shelley correspondence was now printed in *Shelley and Mary*, but the texts were carefully edited: certain names and facts were concealed, and readers were encouraged to consider the story from the family's perspective. And inevitably the few copies of the book would be seen by only a few people. Lady Shelley had not, however, given up on the idea of a full-length biography. In 1883 John Cordy Jeaffreson published *The Real Lord Byron: New Views of the Poet's Life*, in which he dug up the rumour of Shelley's immoral relations with Claire Clairmont. He had found Mary Shelley's refutation among Byron's papers. In July that year, Lady Shelley's friend and neighbour Sir Henry Taylor wrote to Edward Dowden, Professor of English at Trinity College, Dublin: 'The question thus arising has led Percy & Lady Shelley to wish that some acct shd be given of Shelley's life which might represent the truth of it, as disclosed by a large collection of letters & papers which they have had privately printed.'[21] He wondered if Dowden was willing to write this account.

Dowden accepted with enthusiasm, and worked intensively on the book for the next three years. Showing considerable powers of diplomacy, he succeeded in consulting an impressive quantity of primary material. With Garnett's help he persuaded Lady Shelley to show him the archive kept at Boscombe, including, eventually, the Shelley correspondence. Until then he had only known it from the texts printed in *Shelley and Mary*, and in his copy of this book (now in the British Library) he carefully noted the discrepancies between manuscript and transcript. Dowden managed to see the papers that Claire Clairmont had offered to Sir Percy, and which now belonged to the Shelley scholar Harry Buxton Forman. He even saw the notebook of early Shelley poems that belonged to the children of the poet's daughter by Harriet, Ianthe. Lady Shelley had once invited Ianthe into her Sanctum, and briefly won her over:

> I took her up to my sanctum and showed her the monument to Mary and Shelley. Then I opened the case containing my precious belongings – they are not all there now, I gave a great many away to the Bodleian – and, after opening the *Journal*, I showed her the letter and some of her father's belongings. I then left her alone for an hour. On my return I found her bathed in tears and sobbing bitterly. She had been touched; she knew her father a little bit at last. 'Send my children to me,' she said; 'let them come and love him too.'

Unfortunately, Lady Shelley added, Ianthe's clergyman, 'a narrow episcopalian', had told her that she had done wrong and been led astray. They never saw each other again.[22]

When it came to the all-important question of Shelley's treatment of Harriet, Dowden tried to be as judicious as possible: 'That no act of Shelley's during the two years which immediately preceded her death caused the rash act which brought her life to a close, seems certain.' Inevitably, Lady Shelley was not altogether pleased with Dowden's treatment of the matter, and Garnett had to remind Sir Percy: 'In estimating Professor Dowden's work we must always remember that he is not writing as an advocate, as I did in the Relics, but as an historian – & that it is a great gain to have the favourable verdict of a competent and impartial judge; even if it does not go quite so far as one would wish.'[23] Dowden only threatened to become difficult once. On hearing that a life of Mary Shelley had also been commissioned, from Mrs Florence Marshall, he insisted that he be allowed to publish the manuscript material first, for his biography, surely, was the more important work.

Edward Dowden's biography of Shelley was published in 1886, Florence Marshall's life of Mary Shelley in 1889. Later that year Sir Percy Shelley died. William Michael Rossetti sent Lady Shelley a letter of condolence on behalf of the Shelley Society, honouring Sir Percy as one whose descent, 'if not more than illustrious as coming from Percy Bysshe Shelley, would still have been pre-eminent as derived from a Godwin, a Mary Wollstonecraft, & a Mary Shelley. With this exceptional dignity of descent were combined the many loveable & honourable qualities of the man himself.'[24] Lady Shelley now thought seriously about the future custody of the family archive. Stimulated by the biographical activity, she and Sir Percy had gone on adding to it. Sometime before 1887 they had purchased the manuscripts of *Frankenstein* from a Mr. A.H. Bradford, who had obtained them from 'a picture-cleaner named Godwin'. The name seems too good to be true. In the 1880s they had acquired the letters Mary Wollstonecraft had written to Henry Fuseli, which Godwin had failed to see. Having looked over them, Sir Percy decided that they were not particularly interesting. There were rumours that other manuscripts had been consigned to the flames at Boscombe Manor.

Richard Garnett advised Lady Shelley to leave Shelley's manuscripts to an institution, 'considering the chances and changes to which private property is always liable'.[25] He tended towards the British Museum, but thought that, as a public institution, they would be less inclined to observe the restrictions that Lady Shelley wanted, than a private library such as, for instance, the Bodleian. In January 1891 Lady Shelley began her correspondence with Benjamin Jowett. It is not known for certain at what point she decided to divide the papers, but she had noticed with approval that her husband's cousins (descended from the poet's younger brother John) were at last beginning to take an interest in the poet. She eventually decided to divide the Shelley papers and relics between the Bodleian and John C.E. Shelley (later Sir John Shelley-Rolls). John Shelley would receive most of the poet's working notebooks. The remainder of the family archive passed to the sons of her adopted daughter Bessie ('Floss') and her husband Leopold Scarlett, who had died in 1888. This included Godwin's and Mary Wollstonecraft's papers, the Shelleys' incoming correspondence, and three major treasures: Godwin's journal, Mary's journal, and the surviving manuscripts of *Frankenstein*. It also included, in the form of letters and memoranda, Lady Shelley's long battle to preserve, enhance and control the family archive.

Lady Shelley died in 1899. She was buried in the churchyard of St Peter's in Bournemouth, alongside Sir Percy and Mary Shelley. After Mary's death she had had William Godwin's and Mary Wollstonecraft's remains disinterred from St Pancras Churchyard and buried with their daughter. The most precious relic of all, the remains of Shelley's heart, had been buried with Sir Percy.

In 1922, the centenary of Shelley's death, the restricted box of papers was opened. It was found to contain little unpublished material, but the numerous letters therein could now, at least, be compared with the not always faithful versions published in *Shelley and Mary*, and those included, wholly or in part, in Dowden's biography. Lady Shelley's demand that the papers could only be consulted with the consent of the Bodleian Library's governing body of Curators stood until 1992, when a bicentenary exhibition of Shelley's manuscripts, first editions and relics, *Shelley's Guitar*, provided a suitable occasion for this by now pointless restriction to be lifted. In 1946 Sir John Shelley-Rolls presented the Shelley notebooks to the Bodleian, and bequeathed the remainder of his Shelley papers and relics to the Library. They were received in 1961. The Scarlett brothers, Shelley and Robert, who had inherited the residual papers, became the 5th and 6th Barons Abinger. In 2004 the 'Abinger Papers' were purchased by the Bodleian from the 9th Baron Abinger. The Boscombe archive was thus reunited.

In November 1818 Shelley had visited the public library in Ferrara, where he saw the manuscripts of the sixteenth-century Italian poets Ariosto and Tasso. 'I could fancy Ariosto sitting in it', he wrote to Thomas Love Peacock on seeing the poet's armchair, '& the satires in his own hand writing which they unfold beside it, & the old bronze inkstand loaded with figures which belonged also to him assists the willing delusion.' Ariosto's handwriting, he thought, expressed 'a strong & keen but circumscribed energy of mind'. He also saw some of Tasso's manuscripts, and found in them evidence of 'an intense & earnest mind exceeding at times its own depth'. 'You know I always seek in what I see the manifestation of something beyond the present & tangible object', he told Peacock.[26] Whatever we seek today, ghostly or not, beyond the present, tangible manuscripts of Shelley, Mary Shelley, William Godwin and Mary Wollstonecraft, there is no disputing their intellectual riches, and their continuing hold over the imagination.

Scenic, Poesy & Thought

Leave thy lamps...

of the dwellers of a cot

Bright & ...

❧ 9 ❧

Sparks and Ashes:
Shelley's Poetry Manuscripts outside Bodley

Elizabeth Campbell Denlinger

O thou, who chariotest to their dark wintry bed
The winged seeds, where they lie cold and low,
Each like a corpse within its grave...
Scatter, as from an unextinguished hearth,
Ashes and sparks, my words among mankind!

Percy Bysshe Shelley, *Ode to the West Wind*

Manuscripts are peculiarly potent objects. Their power is primarily realized by printing, by the spread of meaning. In regard to this power, Shelley's metaphor of the seed is apt. His ambitions lifelong aimed at fostering growth – political, moral and intellectual – in his readers. After a writer's death, however, his or her manuscripts begin to exert the more intimate power of the relic, which is what draws collectors to them. At the same time, the death of the author confers the authority of finality which scholars value. For both of these groups, manuscripts possess the power of changing time. In the collector, a manuscript enables travel to the past, the chance to see and grasp in imagination the hands that wrote; it arouses wonder at the survival of something so easily destroyed. For editors and scholars, working from manuscripts has an opposite effect: although they are hardly impervious to the wish to travel back in time, for them the manuscript (published or not) is a live instrument, its meaning not yet, or no longer, settled. A scholar at work sees the manuscript come forth to the present and throw itself into the future once again. Beyond these general observations, we may remark that Shelley's personal charisma – transferable and adhesive, like an unguent – did not die with him but attaches to everything he touched and most of all to the products of his pen.

II.   QUEEN MAB.   29

All knowledge of the past revived; the events
   Of old and wondrous times,
Which dim tradition interruptedly
Teaches the credulous vulgar, were unfolded
   In just perspective to the view;
   Yet dim from their infinitude.
     The Spirit seemed to stand
High on an isolated pinnacle;
The flood of ages combating below,
The depth of the unbounded universe
     Above, and all around
   Nature's unchanging harmony.

flood

Necessity's

There is an element of chance in the survival of any manuscript, especially of those prepared for the press. For much of the history of printing, once a text was correctly set, the author's manuscript became superfluous: the grain winnowed, the manuscript was so much chaff. Many of Shelley's ended up on the granary floor. As one of his editors remarks:

> The curious thing about Shelley's literary manuscripts is not the number which have survived but the number which have disappeared. It seems almost incredible, for instance, that there should be no manuscript of *The Cenci* or of *Alastor*, or such other of his major works as *Adonais*, *Epipsychidion*, or *Hellas*. No one would expect Shelley to keep such manuscripts for he seldom kept anything, including letters; but Mary Shelley … kept so many manuscripts [that] the loss of the rest seems strange.[1]

Of the manuscripts that survived, the greater part remained with Mary Shelley, and after her death in 1851 with her son and daughter-in-law Sir Percy Florence and Jane, Lady Shelley. The Bodleian benefited more than any other institution by this familial custody, as the preceding pages have shown; the reunion of these manuscripts is the occasion for this volume. But others were scattered to the world. Desirable manuscripts seldom move randomly. They are subject to the centrifugal force of the market and the centripetal force of the institution, and the flow of philanthropy in the twentieth century, according to which collectors often leave their possessions to their schools or favourite museums or libraries, has allowed the latter force to win out: all of Shelley's known extant literary manuscripts are now in institutional hands.

Shelley's ghost, in its papery forms, has given rise to a number of stories, some amusing, some chilling, their actors often displaying actions and minds that are most unShelleyan. It is the task of this essay to tell some of these stories. I am concerned with the literary manuscripts of Percy Bysshe Shelley and even with this limitation make no pretence to completeness. Rather, I have shamelessly focused on those manuscripts whose narratives promised the greatest interest. The straightforward provenance of the Huntington notebooks, for instance, important as they are – they are those that Shelley used during his life in Italy – will not be given at length. (But here it is in brief: Sir Percy and Lady Shelley gave them to their friend, the Shelley scholar and advocate Richard Garnett. Garnett died in 1906 and a St Louis collector, William Keeney Bixby, purchased them at the sale of his books. In 1918 Bixby sold them to Henry Huntington, and they have remained ever since at Huntington's magnificent library.)

Figure 77 P.B. Shelley, revisions and doodles on *Queen Mab*. New York Public Library, Pforzheimer Collection of Shelley and His Circle.

The Two Mabs (British Library)

In 1905 Thomas James Wise (1859–1937) purchased a copy of *Queen Mab*
annotated by Shelley, which did nothing to salve the envy he felt for
his friend and accomplice Harry Buxton Forman's better copy with
extensive draft revisions. In his bibliography of the Ashley Library (its
plummy name taken from a London street where Wise briefly resided)
he minimized the differences. Wise's copy is now in the British Library.
The superior one that belonged to Forman (1842–1917) resides at the Carl
H. Pforzheimer Collection of Shelley and His Circle of the New York
Public Library. A home in America was precisely the fate from which
Forman tried to save it.

Soon after the 1813 printing of his first major poem, *Queen Mab*,
P.B. Shelley was convinced when both printer and publisher refused
to put their names on it that the work's radical politics would lead to
prosecution. He withdrew the book from circulation, though he privately
distributed a considerable number of copies. It remained technically
unpublished during his lifetime, but was nonetheless pirated first in
1821 becoming immensely popular with British radicals throughout the
nineteenth century, particularly for its incendiary republican notes. For
himself, Shelley made use of two printed copies to revise the poem,
writing directly on its pages. Of the more extensively used copy we know
a good deal: in early 1818 he left the house where he had been living
since 1817 in Marlow, Buckinghamshire, and went to Italy with Claire
Clairmont and Mary Shelley. He left his furniture and debts behind
him, and the book passed to his landlord. Its provenance can be traced
thereafter without a break, but the part of its story that concerns us
begins in 1896 when Harry Buxton Forman bought it for £6.[2]

Wise and Forman have been so long in disgrace now that it is
difficult to remember the exalted positions they once held in British
bibliography. Forman's scholarship still commands respect: 'his [Shelley]
editions remain the most carefully proofread and accurate (according
to the evidence available to him) that have ever been produced'.[3]
Forman's role as forger is thus both ironic and comprehensible: expert
in – indeed preoccupied with – bibliographical variation, he saw how
it would be possible to create forgeries without an original. He and
Wise found obscure and juvenile works from established poets and
issued them in pamphlets purporting to be hitherto unknown (or,
oxymoronically, hitherto forgotten) editions. The most famous was
an edition of Elizabeth Barrett Browning's *Sonnets from the Portuguese*.
From 1887 into the early years of the twentieth century, they produced
dozens of forgeries, which they sold to fellow collectors, using the
proceeds to enlarge their collections. Forman, an administrator at

the Post Office, had much to lose by the enterprise. Yet the idea was his.[4]

Thomas J. Wise was a successful dealer in essential oils – lavender, bergamot, vanillin, ylang-ylang and the like; though entirely self-taught, he attained considerable esteem in British and American bibliophilic circles. Shelley was his darling as well as Forman's, though it was an affection they shared with many readers and collectors of the day. It was Wise who made forgery a business, using his expertise and reputation to make their productions credible, respectable, and all too available.

The two men were themselves passionate collectors; Forman wrote to a friend in 1886 that he had 'got the fever very bad'.[5] Wise for his part writes like a schoolboy to Forman of a proposed swap: 'If you want a real fine Borrow MS or two, as you say, you had better bring a real fine Shelley Letter with you!!!!!! One of the "good 'uns"! – Now don't tell me I'm never greedy!"[6] No one would ever have told Wise such a thing. But Wise and Forman are not unrepresentative of their generation, which had boundless enthusiasm for book collecting.

Their criminal partnership was uneasy, and its discomforts are demonstrated in the correspondence between the two men when the second annotated *Queen Mab* appeared. This copy's early history is uncertain, but it went unsold at a Sotheby's auction in 1905, and in September of that year it appeared on the shelves of a bookdealer named Frank Sabin. Wise wrote to Forman and told him about it in such a way that it appeared he was not pursuing the book himself. When Wise did buy *Mab*, Forman wrote him a letter opening: 'I cannot say that the tone of your letter of today surprised me – nothing does that.... But somehow I regret it. Why didn't you tell me you were in for the Q.M.?' He goes on to describe Wise's tone as 'accusatory' and asks if Wise expected him 'to lie, & say that I thought it was a duffer' (i.e. spurious, which would have pressed Sabin to drop the price) – 'I don't think you can have expected that, as you know, or should know, that is not my way.' One is reminded that being a criminal is no impediment to feeling oneself essentially honest. Forman closes handsomely, congratulating Wise on having 'saved it from going to America', and calling its £350 price 'dirt cheap'.[7]

The two brought the manuscripts together for comparison a few weeks later, and in October Forman published an article on them in the *Athenæum*. In 1911 Wise offered Forman £1,000 for his *Queen Mab* and his copy of *Laon and Cythna*, also revised by Shelley: 'The two "Mabs" ought to reside in company forever.' Forman refused, writing 'No possible offence but don't feel I can do without the 2 books, tho' at present I can do without the sum they represent.'[8]

Wise tried once more to acquire the better copy. When Forman died in 1917, Wise helped to sort through his magnificent collection. A Mr Mudie from the bookselling firm of Bernard Quaritch was primarily responsible for this task. On the way out one evening he accidentally put on Wise's coat and (in John Collins's telling) discovered, nestled in the pocket, the annotated *Queen Mab*. Wise appeared just as Mudie discovered his mistake. "'Were you taking that home?" he asked Wise as they exchanged coats. "Thought I'd look it over" Wise explained, flustered only for a moment. "Quite forgot I had it." He replaced it, chuckling genially."[9]

Wise was apparently willing to steal the book, but when he had the chance to purchase it at the 1920 sale of Forman's library at the Anderson Galleries in New York, he passed. Something in his drive to acquire failed; or perhaps something about buying from Americans put him off. He had the money, and would certainly have been able to employ an agent to bid for him. In the event, *Queen Mab* went to the legendary Dr A.S.W. Rosenbach of Philadelphia; he sold it to the composer Jerome Kern, who was briefly an important collector. At the Kern Sale of 1929 it went for a record $68,000 – but languished, after the stock-market crash, in the offices of the New York dealer Gabriel Wells. After Wells's death in 1951, Carl H. Pforzheimer bought it for $8,000.[10] The copy of *Laon and Cythna* with Shelley's revisions is six blocks south and one avenue east of the New York Public Library at the Morgan Library & Museum, still formally known as the Pierpont Morgan Library.

Wise and Forman's forgeries, long suspected, were definitively proven in 1934 by John Carter and Graham Pollard's *Enquiry into the Nature of Certain Nineteenth Century Pamphlets*.[11] Happily for Forman, he had been dead seventeen years; his son Maurice, who had published a few false imprints himself, did not have an easy time of it. Wise had a greater capacity for bad faith than either of the Formans – his conscience was brass through and through – and he never confessed. At his death he stipulated only that his collection should be offered first to the British Museum (now the British Library) and that it not be put up for auction in the United States.

Wise's widow sold the Ashley Library to the British Museum for a sum considerably below its market value and threw in the shelves for free (they were afterwards found to be 'the thinnest veneer over plain deal'[11]). The books were given a room of their own where they remain; 'Ashley' is still their shelfmark.

The Scrope Davies Notebook (British Library)

While it is true that in general desirable manuscripts don't often move at random, occasionally they do; perhaps more often they remain randomly at rest for decades or centuries. This is the case with another significant Shelley holding of the British Library: a notebook containing early drafts of two important poems, *Mont Blanc* and *Hymn to Intellectual Beauty*, as well as two sonnets unknown until the trunk was noticed in the basement of the Pall Mall branch of Barclay's Bank in 1976.

Shelley had published political pamphlets and *Alastor and Other Poems*, but he was still relatively unknown in the summer of 1816 when these poems were composed during a visit to Geneva. It was a significant sojourn, shared with Byron, Claire Clairmont and Mary Godwin,[12] and now most famous for spawning *Frankenstein*. Shelley – we don't know if it was accidental or purposeful – left his notebook with Byron when he returned to England in August. Byron's friend Scrope Davies followed him only few days later.

Why Davies neglected to return the notebook to Shelley is unknown. A colourful figure, Davies was unfortunately omitted from the *Dandies* series of cigarette cards issued by Players in the 1930s, despite the presence of his friends Lord Byron and Beau Brummell. Possibly his sudden disappearance from the London scene, occasioned by gambling debts that threatened prison, accounts for it; his later life in Europe was obscure. He is more lastingly memorialized in the pages of Byron's letters. Yet it was the discovery of his trunk, left behind at his Pall Mall banker's offices in 1820 when Davies fled, that renewed his fame and enabled his biography to be written. The trunk contained most of the papers of Davies's life up to that point: financial records, academic papers, legal documents, correspondence (including his letters from Byron), a commonplace book, a cellar book, and notes on gambling strategies.[13] The plum was the third canto of *Childe Harold's Pilgrimage*, which Davies had, as instructed by Byron, taken to Byron's publisher John Murray. Since Murray had already set it in type from another copy – one carried, in fact, by Shelley – Davies kept it. Collectors were, thus, never part of the chain of these manuscripts' transmission: Davies's descendants generously placed the trunk and its contents on permanent loan to the British Library, where it remains.

The Silsbee Notebooks (Houghton Library, Harvard University)

The story of the two Shelley notebooks given by Edward Silsbee to Harvard will return us, eventually, to Harry Buxton Forman. But Forman is the end of this story, which is probably the most familiar in this essay as it furnished the germ of Henry James's *Aspern Papers*, his novella centred on an editor's pursuit of a charismatic American poet's papers carefully hoarded by his former mistress. James's tale – in which the letters come to an ashen end – is, well, masterful. Yet there is another tale altogether to be told about the women and, peripherally, the men who lived the fleshly version.

The tale begins with Claire Clairmont, third partner and fifth wheel in the ménage of Percy Bysshe and Mary Shelley and their children. Her earlier life has been sketched elsewhere in these pages. After Shelley's death she became – what else? – a governess, and later a paid companion. In this capacity she lived in Russia, Austria, Italy, England, finally returning to Italy where she settled. From the mid-1860s until her death in March 1879, she lived in Florence, haunted by thoughts of Allegra, her daughter by Lord Byron, who had taken custody of the child and placed her for education in a convent in Bagnacavallo. Allegra learned to read and write, and died there, aged five, in April 1822. In Claire Clairmont's retirement this death became the central fact of life, one she couldn't always acknowledge: there were times when she insisted that Allegra was still alive, spirited off somewhere.[14] In her telling, Byron's character is flattened into an incarnate evil and the events leading to Allegra's death a melodrama. Reading through her recollections written in the 1870s one is struck by this flatness above all, by the beggared imagination of one whose thoughts have been squandered on a useless object.

It was into Claire's Florence palazzo that her niece Pauline Clairmont entered. The eldest of seven, Pauline – known as Plin – had been in contact with her Aunt Claire from the 1850s onward and lived with her from 1870 to Claire's death. Plin had been raised in Austria where her father, Claire's brother Charles, was professor of English at the University of Vienna. Pauline herself excelled in music and languages; in her journals she moves 'almost unconsciously from one language to another, as though the European languages were all one to her'.[15] She resembled her aunt in being polyglot and in bearing a daughter out of wedlock.

If history repeats tragedy as farce, familial stories often carry on as melodrama across the generations. Both Claire and Plin transgressed the sexual mores of their time; both paid the price (or won the prize) of remaining unmarried. But Plin's story is resolutely happy where Claire's is resolutely cast down. Marion Stocking, the scholar best acquainted with her life, describes her thus: 'Her journals reveal her as an emancipated woman – freedom-loving, high-spirited, and exuberantly sexual. [They show her] devoted to her brother and his children, deeply responsive to music … fond of horseback riding, drinking, smoking, traveling and …

Figure 79 *right* Pauline
(Plin) Clairmont 1825–1891,
niece of Claire Clairmont,
c.1880s, in a portrait
handed down through
her brother's family.
Probably taken after
her aunt's death, this is
approximately how she
would have appeared
in her dealings with
Silsbee and Forman. New
York Public Library,
Pforzheimer Collection of
Shelley and His Circle.

Figure 80 *far right* P.B.
Shelley, *To a Skylark*. The
notebook Silsbee obtained
from Pauline or Claire
Clairmont preserves fair
copies of some of Shelley's
best-loved lyrics, including
To a Skylark. Houghton
Library, Harvard
University.

literature.'[16] We don't know if her buoyant nature kept her afloat when
her daughter Georgina died at twenty-one, but her sense of adventure
rebounded; Plin would die in 1891 in a mountain-climbing accident.

The woman whom Edward Augustus Silsbee encountered when he
came to the crumbling palazzo in 1872 was, thus, someone very different
from the sheltered creature whom James portrays in *The Aspern Papers*'
Miss Tina. She is also different from the desperate spinster implied by
the stories of Silsbee's having to extricate himself from her schemes of
marriage. On the contrary, Pauline wrote of herself in her journals
in 1859: 'Au fond, je suis née pour être courtisane mais non levée à ce
métier.'[17] It is clear from her journals that she did propose marriage to
him. When Silsbee refused – one suspects she sought respectability more
for her daughter than for herself – they became, briefly, lovers.

Silsbee's object of worship was Shelley; he quoted him constantly
and called him 'the Christ of Literature'.[18] Between 1872 and 1876 he
lodged with the Clairmont ménage, not constantly but for months at
a time. This included Plin's daughter Georgina, seven in 1872 and the

(100)

To a Sky-Lark.

Hail to thee blithe Spirit!
  Bird thou never wert,
That from heaven or near it,
    Pourest thy full heart
In profuse strains of unpremeditated art.
                                    ——— insert

  In the golden lightning
    Of the sunken Sun —
Oer which clouds are brightening
    Thou dost
  Thy wings float & run;
Like an unbodied joy whose race is just begun

  The pale purple even
    Melts around thy flight,
  Like a Star of Heaven
    In the broad daylight   shrill
Thou art unseen, — but yet I hear thy blithe
                                    delight

object of intense competition between her mother and her great aunt. He conversed with Claire by the hour about Byron and the Shelleys, taking notes; and, as we have noted, became differently entangled with Pauline.

The two notebooks he acquired were copy books, 'unique among major institutional collections in consisting primarily of fair copies.'[19] The larger of the two contains about twenty-five poems, copied fair in the hands of both Percy Bysshe and Mary Shelley, among them *To a Skylark*, republican poems written after the Peterloo Massacre of 1819, a translation from Moschus, and Shelley's letter-poem to Lady Mount Cashell, *The Sensitive Plant*. It was already on deposit at Harvard in 1877, and it seems likely that Silsbee had acquired both at once on one of his sojourns. It is unclear whether it was Claire or Pauline Clairmont, or both, who made the gift to him. Annotations by both Claire Clairmont and Silsbee to the second notebook imply that the aunt and not the niece gave him at least this notebook.[20]

In any case, after Claire Clairmont's death in 1879 – dolorous and self-pitying to the end, she left directions that her tomb be inscribed 'In misery she spend [*sic*] her life expiating not only her faults but also her virtues' – the real contest began.[21] To follow it fully would lead me beyond the boundaries of Shelley's poetical manuscripts. In brief, though: Harry Buxton Forman quickly had representatives on the spot. Silsbee had arrived in February, before Claire's death. Her will left the bulk of her slender estate in trust for Georgina, so it should be remembered that Plin was acting throughout not only on her own behalf but on her daughter's.

She certainly acted beyond her authority. Claire had appointed an executor, Bartolomeo Cini, the son-in-law of Lady Mount Cashell, and when he died she appointed his son Giovanni. (Lady Mount Cashell – in full, Margaret King Moore Tighe – was the mother of Nerina Tighe Cini and connected the generations: in girlhood she was the pupil of Mary Wollstonecraft and as an adult, settled in Italy, the steadfast friend to both Shelleys and to Claire Clairmont.) Florence and Pistoia, where the Cinis lived (and live) are about 47 kilometres apart, not then a convenient distance. Perhaps this accounts for the way things fell out, or perhaps Giovanni Cini was for some other reason unable to carry out his duties. In any case Pauline took charge of the estate. The customary way to see this story has been to set at odds her love for Silsbee and her avarice. But it seems far more likely that her heart was more invested in her daughter's well-being than her own romantic adventures, especially since Silsbee seemed to have bowed out. He had no cash in any case, and when Forman's representatives offered £150 for the papers, she gave them most of what they wanted – though not quite.

Forman had expected in his hoard letters from Edward Trelawny (the adventurer and friend of Shelley's and Byron's who more than once offered his hand to Claire), a miniature of Allegra, and the larger manuscript notebook. He himself travelled to Vienna later where he gave Pauline another sum for the first two of these. Eventually, she gave him Shelley's inkstand as well, which Claire had left to Giovanni Cini, and which she had traded to him for a portrait of Lady Mount Cashell.[22] Forman's total haul was considerable: he had obtained four Shelley notebooks, a prose manuscript on sculpture in Rome and Florence, a copy of the uncommon *Address to the Irish People* (1813), and over 150 letters mostly from Mary Shelley and Percy Bysshe Shelley, including, as well, some from Godwin and Mary Jane Godwin. But he lacked the prize, and the librarians at Harvard were exceedingly ambivalent when in 1889 he requested – strenuously, ready to pay whatever it took – a full transcription. It was never forthcoming. Forman, one doesn't doubt, felt himself deeply cheated all over again.

The Esdaile Notebook (The Carl H. Pforzheimer Collection of Shelley and His Circle, New York Public Library)

The story of the Esdaile Notebook, like that of the Scrope Davies Notebook, contains more stillness than motion. Once in motion, however, it went very quickly from semi-invisibility to full publication with notes and critical apparatus. The notebook remained in the family of Shelley's daughter Eliza Ianthe Shelley Esdaile from late 1813 to 1962, when the Pforzheimer Library acquired it at auction at Sotheby's. In 1964 it was published by Knopf. One of its later editors summed up nicely its trajectory: '[Kenneth Neill] Cameron and the staff of the Carl H. Pforzheimer Library, with strong support from Carl H. Pforzheimer, Jr., and the other officers of the Carl and Lily Pforzheimer Foundation, Inc., and the cooperation of Alfred A. Knopf, had produced in less than two years what Shelley and generations of scholars had struggled in vain since December 1811 to bring to publication.'[23] It contains, as Cameron noted, 'early poems, poems not of fulfillment but of promise'.[24] Shelley submitted them to his publisher, Thomas Hookham, who declined them, and discussed them with his mentor (and later father-in-law) William Godwin, who cautioned against 'indiscriminate early publication'.[25] Later, in a letter to Keats, Shelley called them his 'first blights' and was glad he had failed to publish them. To us they afford an unparalleled view of a poet in formation.

He was also a poet married at nineteen to a girl of sixteen, and this marriage is part of the reason for the book's having remained so long in the privacy of the family. Steeped in the sensibility of the gothic, and possessed of a powerful sense of justice, Shelley had impulses both heroic and chivalric towards young women imprisoned by their fathers. Harriet Westbrook, his sister's schoolfriend, appeared to him to be such a victim. They fell in love, eloped, and married in Scotland where such things were more easily arranged. The marriage produced two children, Ianthe and Charles. During its brief duration Shelley and Harriet were constantly on the move, in England, Wales, and Ireland, partly for financial reasons, and partly because Harriet had thrown in her lot with a poet working as hard as he could in as many ways as he knew to change the world. The titles of some of the poems indicate their political bent: 'To Liberty'; 'On Robert Emmet's tomb'; 'To the Republicans of North America'; 'Sonnet. To a balloon, laden with knowledge'; 'Sonnet. On Launching some bottles'. Both of the last referred to Shelley's unorthodox ways of circulating radical broadsides he had had printed up – in a small hot-air balloon, and thrown in corked bottles into the Bristol Channel.

But the young couple were beset by debt and parental disapproval. During one of their many moves, and owing to his non-payment of a printer's bill, Shelley had to abandon in Dublin the poems that went into what became known as the Esdaile Notebook. He was able to ransom them later, but the anxiety caused by the threat of their loss led to his lifelong habit of keeping copybooks for the safety of his work. Shelley gave this first copybook to Harriet, possibly some time late in 1813, but certainly before he eloped to Europe with Mary Wollstonecraft Godwin in July 1814. He invited Harriet to live with them in a vaguely sororal, vaguely uxorial arrangement, but to her the prospect was somehow unappealing. Harriet Shelley's reaction was exactly what one might expect of a very young mother of two inexplicably abandoned by a husband with whom she was still in love. She committed suicide in late 1816, begging her sister, Eliza, to take care of Ianthe. It was probably through Eliza that Ianthe was given the notebook.

Of the six children we know Percy Bysshe Shelley to have begotten, only two, Ianthe and Percy Florence, lived to adulthood. Ianthe's later life was just as respectable and nearly as comfortable as that of her baronet half-brother. The Westbrooks and later the Esdailes, understandably, had a very different relationship to the memory of the great poet, especially after Sir Percy and Lady Shelley connived at Shelley's early biographer's efforts to besmirch Harriet Shelley's name. (She was pregnant by another man when she died.) For decades the notebook was known to researchers; in his authorized biography of Shelley (1886) Edward Dowden published a few of the poems. (Lest you fear that Wise and Forman do not enter this story, be advised that their first forgery – generally considered their best – was a volume titled *Poems and Sonnets*, comprising the poems that Dowden had published, and pirating much of his scholarship in the apparatus.[26]) But the family refused to let the whole be published. From Ianthe Esdaile the notebook passed in 1876 to her daughter Eliza Margaret Esdaile, who 'placed the Notebook for safekeeping with her brother, Charles Edward Jeffries Esdaile'.[27] Eliza Margaret Esdaile left it to her niece, Lettice Esdaile Worrall, who sold it. The purchase was a great event for the Pforzheimer Library, then administered by Carl H. Pforzheimer, Jr. The volume fetched considerably less at auction than one might have expected, because Sotheby's had mistakenly advertised that rights to publish the volume rested with the Oxford University Press – whereas in fact the Press had merely non-exclusive permission.[28] In 1962 there were no regulations on exports of national treasures; nor were minute inspections of one's person or one's luggage customary. Nonetheless, the safety of the notebook had to be ensured, and Pforzheimer's daughter, returning to the United States with her children and husband, took charge of it in her personal luggage.

Of the Carl H. Pforzheimer Collection of Shelley and His Circle as a whole a few words are due, since outside the Bodleian its holdings are the richest of any Shelley collection in the world. Until 1986, the collection was only a major component of the Carl H. Pforzheimer Library, best known for its rich collection of English literature 1475–1700 (including Shakespeare quartos and all four folios, and Milton's *Comus* with his annotations), but which held many other treasures as well, not least a complete Gutenberg Bible.

The library was first housed in the family's Park Avenue apartment, and later moved to offices at 41 East 42nd Street, chosen for their proximity to the New York Public Library. The first Carl H. Pforzheimer (1879–1957) was the prime mover of the collection and he took an active part in its daily life. His spidery, elegant hand appears constantly in notes in the collection's records. And he was interested in educating New York's potential collectors: in the archives there is an undated group of short essays in prose and verse from the twelfth grade of the Lenox School (a private girls' school), remembering their visit to the Library. The Romantic poets were the stars of the show, but the girls were also impressed by the librarian Emma Unger's talk on bibliography and Mr Pforzheimer's talk on bindings – 'He stated a fact I never knew, the first publishers neglected to put book covers on so it was done by the original owner.'[29] Whether any of them went on to collect books we don't know, but since the Carl and Lily Pforzheimer Foundation donated the collection to the New York Public Library in 1986, those

Figure 82 Carl and Lily Pforzheimer at the grave of E.J. Trelawny, the Protestant Cemetery in Rome. Unidentified photographer, ?1930s. Photographs in the Pforzheimer Collection document the Pforzheimers' travels to sites important to the Shelleys and Byron; here they stand at Trelawny's grave, next to P.B. Shelley's.

who had cared for the collection have continued to make it available for bibliographic education as well as Romantic research.

Shelley and his circle were a significant focus of the Pforzheimer Library from the collection's beginning, some time in the first decade of the twentieth century. Its claim to originality stems from its omnivorous nature: encompassing books and manuscripts of major and minor literary writers of the period, it also includes history, sermons, conduct books, children's books, captivity narratives, chapbooks, tracts, political pamphlets, maps, county histories, books of genealogy – in short, anything that might support research in British Romanticism. In manuscripts, although its holdings in poetry include *Prince Athanase*, fragments of *Laon and Cythna*, and a number of lyric poems, its great strength lies in its letters. The collection has, as well, important prose holdings, most notably the manuscript of *A Philosophical View of Reform*. Beginning in 1961, *Shelley and his Circle* began to appear, publishing selected manuscripts of the collection. (Bruce Rogers, the designer, insisted on the lower case 'h' to fit the spine.) These volumes form a 'bibliographical hybrid: part catalogue, part collective biography, part social history, and part literary criticism'.[30] The collection, now numbering over 10,000 manuscripts and 15,000 books, continues to grow.

Figure 83 Room 319
at the New York Public
Library – the home and
reading room of the
Pforzheimer Collection,
as it is today, with many
of the antique furnishings
from the original
collector's library. Photo:
© Peter Aaron/ Esto

Diaspora

To return to where we began – never was an essay so picaresque, not to say Shandean, as this one – a few notes will convey some of the ways in which some Shelley manuscripts have been scattered. His longest poem, *Laon and Cythna*, for instance, survives in rough drafts in the Bodleian, which also holds the largest part of the fair copy known to survive. But Mary Shelley was in the habit of giving away pieces of the fair copy 'as examples of Shelley's autograph'.[31] Libraries holding fragments of *Laon and Cythna* include, besides the Bodleian: the Pforzheimer Collection, the British Library (Ashley), the National Library of Scotland, the Miriam Lutcher Stark Library of the University of Texas, Trinity College Library in Cambridge, and the W. Luther Lewis Collection of Texas Christian University. To trace the trajectory of each fragment would occupy more space than I have here, but merely pointing to their homes indicates how many frequent-flier miles editors may accumulate in the course of their labours.

Another major event in dispersing Shelley manuscripts was the Harry Buxton Forman sale in March, April and October 1920. Carl H. Pforzheimer, among others, bought largely there. J.P. Morgan acquired the manuscript of *Julian and Maddalo*, which went straight to the Morgan Library where it remains (along with the revised printed copy of *Laon and Cythna*) one of their great treasures. A.S.W. Rosenbach bought almost half of all that was offered, and from Rosenbach the books and manuscripts were further dispersed. It seems most unlikely that Forman would have wished his collection to be disposed of in New York, but apparently he did not leave the same explicit directions that Wise did.

There are minor poetry manuscripts scattered among many of the great, and some of the smaller, libraries in the United States, Britain, and (to a much smaller degree) Europe. These include Aberdeen University Library; the Beinecke Library of Yale University; the Berg Collection of the New York Public Library; the Bibliotheca Bodmeriana in Cologny, Switzerland; the Brotherton Collection at the University of Leeds; Eton College Library; the Isabella Stewart Gardner Museum in Boston; the Rosenbach Museum and Library in Philadelphia; Trinity College, Dublin; and others. The diaspora of minor holdings is largely explained by the fact that they *were* minor, and never part of the family collection, but stayed with early Shelley editors and friends such as Charles Ollier and Leigh Hunt. These were more likely to be have been sold on the open market to collectors who could not acquire on the scale of Carl H. Pforzheimer or J.P. Morgan.

One can't discount altogether the possibility that new Shelley manuscripts will turn up. In 2006, for instance, a copy of his 1811

Poetical Essay on the Existing State of Things was found in Oxfordshire, inscribed with the name of his cousin Pilfold Medwin. To be sure, this is a printed work, but there is no other copy known. One recalls as well the discovery in 1997 of an unpublished story of Mary Shelley, *Maurice or the Fisher's Cot* at the Palazzo Cini in Tuscany, home of the same Cini family to whom Claire Clairmont left Shelley's inkstand. (For that matter, the Pforzheimer Collection owns an unpublished novel, *Selene*, by Lady Mount Cashell. There are said to be other unpublished manuscripts of Lady Mount Cashell's in the Palazzo Cini as well.) And there are works of Shelley's that have apparently been altogether lost: a novel titled *Hubert Cauvin*, designed 'to exhibit the cause of the failure of the French Revolution', for instance, is mentioned in letters of early 1812, but disappears from view.[32] Regardless of possible future discoveries, Shelley's legacy has long since been secured. After a writer's death it is editors, publishers and readers who ensure that the hearth is not extinguished; and these Shelley has never lacked.

Notes

Chapter 1

1. The ceremony was reported in an article in *The Times*, 15 June 1893: 'The Shelley Memorial at Oxford'.
2. See *The Complete Poetry of Percy Bysshe Shelley*, ed. Donald H. Reiman and Neil Fraistat, vol. 1 (Baltimore and London: Johns Hopkins University Press, 2000), pp. 237–8.
3. *Shelley Memorials: from Authentic Sources*, ed. Lady Shelley (London: Smith, Elder & Co., 1859), p. 22.
4. Guido Biagi to Lady Shelley, 14 November 1891; MS. Abinger c. 73, fol. 12.
5. Benjamin Jowett to Lady Shelley, 16 April 1891; MS. Abinger c. 72, fols 151–2.
6. Benjamin Jowett to Lady Shelley, 25 September 1891; MS. Abinger, c. 73, fols 5–7.
7. Benjamin Jowett to Lady Shelley, 30 November 1891; MS. Abinger, c. 73, fols 14–15.
8. Ibid.
9. Benjamin Jowett to Lady Shelley, 11 June 1892; MS. Abinger, c. 73, fols 49–50.
10. Lady Shelley to E.W.B. Nicholson, 23 April 1893; Bodleian Library, Library Records d. 1849, fol. 21.
11. Preface to *Poetry of Byron*, chosen and arranged by Matthew Arnold, 1881. *The Complete Prose Works of Mattew Arnold*, ed. R.H. Super, 11 vols (Ann Arbor: University of Michigan Press, 1973), vol. 9, *English Literature and Irish Politics*, p. 237.
12. 'Shelley and his College', *The Speaker*, vol. 7 (17 June 1893), p.680
13. Lady Shelley to Richard Garnett, 23 May 1894; *Letters about Shelley from the Richard Garnett Papers, University of Texas*, ed. William Thurman, Jr. (Ph. D. thesis, University of Texas at Austin, 1972; Ann Arbor, 1985), Bodleian Library, [printed] Shelley adds. e.27, p.206.

Chapter 2

1. The journal volumes, now in the Bodleian, are shelfmarked MSS. Abinger e. 1–32.
2. *Memoirs of the Author of a Vindication of the Rights of Woman*, ed. Pamela Clemit and Gina Luria Walker (Peterborough Ontario: Broadview, 2001), p. 80.
3. See William St Clair, *The Godwins and the Shelleys* (London: Faber & Faber, 1989), pp. 497–503.
4. Godwin and Wollstonecraft correspondence, 17 August 1796; MS. Abinger c. 40, fols 17–22 (*The Collected Letters of Mary Wollstonecraft*, ed. Janet Todd (London: Allen Lane, 2003), pp. 348–50).

5. MS. Abinger c. 3, fols 104–5.

6. *Posthumous Works of the Author of a Vindication of the Rights of Woman*, 4 vols (London: Joseph Johnson, 1798), vol. 3, Preface.

7. *Memoirs*, p. 43.

8. Ibid., p. 103.

9. Quoted in *Memoirs*, p. 182.

10. Unknown correspondent to Godwin, 26 January 1799; MS. Abinger c. 4, fols 73–4.

11. Maud Rolleston, *Talks with Lady Shelley* (London: G.G. Harrap, 1925), p. 34.

Chapter 3

1. See Pamela Clemit, 'William Godwin and James Watt's Copying Machine: Wet-transfer Copies in the Abinger Papers', *Bodleian Library Record*, vol. xviii, no. 5 (April 2005), pp. 533–60.

2. Mary Robinson to Godwin, 24 August 1800; MS. Abinger b. 1, fols 1–2.

3. Martin Smart to Godwin, 20 November 1800; MS. Abinger c. 6, fols 76–7.

4. William Green Munford to Godwin, 25 November 1800; MS. Abinger c. 6, fols 80–81.

5. Unknown correspondent to Godwin, 30 November 1800; MS. Abinger c. 6, fols 88–9.

6. Godwin to John Lens, 24 September 1823; MS. Abinger c. 19, fols 105–6.

7. Shelley to Godwin, 3 January 1812; MS. Shelley c. 1, fols 52–3 (*The Letters of Percy Bysshe Shelley*, ed. Frederick L. Jones, 2 vols (Oxford: Clarendon Press, 1964), vol. 1, pp. 219–21.

8. *Shelley: The Critical Heritage*, ed. James E. Barcus (London: Routledge & Kegan Paul, 1975), pp. 140–41.

9. Ibid., pp. 140–41.

10. Robert Southey to Shelley, [July 1820] (*Shelley Letters*, vol. 2, pp. 204–5n).

11. Shelley to Robert Southey, 17 August 1820; transcript by Lady Shelley, MS. Shelley c. 1, fol. 385 (*Shelley Letters*, vol. 2, pp. 230–33).

12. Robert Southey to Shelley, [? September 1820] (*Shelley Letters*, vol. 2, pp. 232–3n).

13. Shelley to Godwin, 16 January 1812; MS. Shelley c. 1, fols 54–5 (*Shelley Letters*, vol. 1, pp. 227–9).

14. Godwin to Shelley, 4 March 1812; MS. Abinger c. 19, fols 37–41.

15. Shelley to Godwin, 8 March 1812; MS. Shelley c. 1, fols 62–3 (*Shelley Letters*, vol. 1, pp. 266–9).

16. Godwin to Shelley, 14 March 1812; MS. Abinger c. 19, fols 42–3.

17. Godwin to Shelley, *c.* 4 July 1812; MS. Abinger c. 19, fols 48–9.

18. *Shelley's Lost Letters to Harriet*, ed. Leslie Hotson (London: Faber & Faber, 1930), pp. 12–13.

19. Shelley to Harriet Shelley, 19 August 1814; MS. Shelley c. 1, fols 96–7 (*Shelley Letters*, vol. 1, pp. 391–3).

20. Mary Shelley to Shelley, 24 October 1814; MS. Shelley c. 1, fols 129–30 (*The Letters of Mary Wollstonecraft Shelley*, ed. Betty T. Bennett, 3 vols (Baltimore: Johns Hopkins University Press, 1980–88), vol. 1, pp. 1–2).

21. Shelley to Mary Shelley, ?25 October 1814; MS. Shelley c. 1, fols 114–15 (*Shelley Letters*, vol. 1, p. 411).

22. Fanny Imlay to Shelley and Mary Shelley, 19 May 1816; MS. Shelley c. 1, fols 154–5 (*The Clairmont Correspondence*, ed. Marion Kingston Stocking, 2 vols (Baltimore, 1995), vol. 1, pp. 47–51).

23. Fanny Imlay to Mary Shelley, 29 July 1816; MS. Shelley c. 1, fols 152–3, 162–3 (*Clairmont Correspondence*, vol. 1, pp. 54–62).

24. Fanny Imlay to Mary Shelley, 3 October 1816; MS. Shelley c. 1, fols 160–61, 164 (*Clairmont Correspondence*, vol. 1, pp. 80–83).

25. Godwin to Shelley, 13 October 1816; MS. Abinger c. 66, fols 18–19.

26. Shelley to Mary, 11 January 1817; MS. Shelley adds. b. 2, fols 85–7 (*Shelley Letters*, vol. 1, pp. 526–9).

27. Godwin to Shelley, 31 January 1818; MS. Abinger c. 66, fols 38–9.

28. Shelley to Godwin, 7 August 1820 (draft); fol. 5 (of 5) MS. Abinger c. 67, fol. 52; fols 1–4, W.L Lewis Collection, Texas Christian University Library (*Shelley Letters*, vol. 2, 224–9).

29. Shelley to Mary Shelley, 18 August 1818; MS. Shelley c. 1, fols 239–40 (*Shelley Letters*, vol. 2, pp. 32–4).

30. Shelley to Mary Shelley, 23 August 1818; MS Shelley c. 1, fols 241–4 (*Shelley Letters*, vol. 2, pp. 34–8).

31. Godwin to Mary Shelley, 9 September 1819; MS. Abinger c. 45, fol. 18.

32. Rolleston, *Talks with Lady Shelley*, pp. 34–5.

33. Lord Byron to Shelley, 25 August 1820; MS. Shelley c. 1, fol. 387.

34. MS. Abinger c. 69, fol. 1.

35. Shelley to Mary Shelley, 7 August 1821; MS. Shelley c. 1, fols 440–42 (*Shelley Letters*, vol. 2, pp. 316–20).

36. Mary Shelley to Shelley, 10 August 1821; MS. Shelley c. 1, fol. 471; (*Mary Shelley Letters*, vol. 1, pp. 204–5).

37. Quoted by Mary Shelley in a letter to Maria Gisborne, *c.* 27 August 1822; MS. Shelley c. 1, fols 521–3 (*Mary Shelley Letters*, vol. 1, pp. 252–6).

38. Shelley to Mary Shelley, 4 July 1822; MS. Shelley c. 1, fols 504–5 (*Shelley Letters*, vol. 2, p. 444).

39. Godwin to Mary Shelley, 6 August 1822; MS. Abinger c. 45, fols 131–2 (*Shelley Letters*, vol. 2, pp. 443–5).

40. Shelley to John and Maria Gisborne, 19 July 1821; MS. Shelley c. 1, fols 432–3 (*Shelley Letters*, vol. 2, p. 310)

Chapter 4

1. Shelley to Godwin, 24 February 1812; MS. Shelley c. 1, fols 60–61 (*Shelley Letters*, i, pp. 258–60.

2. [printed] Shelley e.1.

3. [printed] Shelley e.3.

4. Shelley to Thomas Love Peacock, ?11 January 1822; MS. Shelley c. 1, fols 490–91 (*Shelley Letters*, vol. 1, pp. 373–4).

5. Charles Ollier to Mary Shelley, 17 November 1823; MS. Abinger c. 46, fols 126–7.

6. Mary Shelley to Maria Gisborne, *c.* 19 February 1820; MS. Abinger d. 20, fols 23r-24r (*Mary Shelley Letters*, vol. 1, pp. 128–9).

7. MS. Shelley adds. c. 4, fol. 292r (*Shelley Letters*, vol. 2, pp. 277-8).

8. Journal entry, 2 October 1822 (*Mary Shelley Journals*, vol. 2, pp. 429–30).

9. Mary Shelley to Lord Byron, ?25 February 1823 (*Mary Shelley Letters*, vol. 1, pp. 315–16).

10. Shelley to Charles Ollier, 16 February 1821 (*Shelley Letters*, vol. 1, pp. 262–3).

11. Charles Ollier to Mary Shelley, 17 November 1823; MS. Abinger c. 46, fols 126–7.

12. Shelley to John Gisborne, 18 June 1822 (*Shelley Letters*, vol. 1, pp. 434–7).

13. MS. Shelley adds. e. 12.

14. MS. Shelley adds. e. 9.

15. MS. Shelley d. 1.

16. MS. Shelley adds. e. 6.

17. MS. Shelley adds. e. 8.

Chapter 5

1. *Blackwoods Edinburgh Magazine*, vol. 2, no. 12 (March 1818), p. 613; *Quarterly Review*, vol. 18, no. 36 (January 1818), p. 382.

2. Claire Clairmont to Edward Trelawny, 21 September 1875 (*Clairmont Correspondence*, vol. 2, pp. 630–33).

3. Shelley to Thomas Love Peacock, 25 July 1818 (*Shelley Letters*, vol. 2, pp. 23–7).

4. Journal entry for 29 July 1814; MS. Abinger d. 27, fol. 2r. (*Mary Shelley Journals*. vol. 1, p. 7).

5. Journal entry, 21 August 1816; *Mary Shelley Journals*, vol. 1, p. 130.

6. Mary Shelley to Shelley, 5 December 1816; MS. Shelley c. 1, fols 146–7 (*Mary Shelley Letters*, vol. 1, pp. 22–4).

7. *The Manuscripts of the Younger Romantics, Shelley*, vol. 9, *The Frankenstein Notebooks*, ed. Charles E. Robinson, 2 vols (New York & London: Garland, 1996) vol. 1, pp. 10–11.

8. *Mary Shelley Journals*, vol. 1, p. 171.

9. Shelley to Charles Ollier, 3 August 1818 (*Shelley Letters*, vol. 1, p. 549).

10. Shelley to Charles Ollier, 8 August 1817 (*Shelley Letters*, vol. 1, p. 552).

11. Shelley to Lackington, Allen & Co., 22 August 1817 (*Shelley Letters*, vol. 1, p. 553).

12. Shelley to Walter Scott, 2 January 1818 (*Shelley Letters*, vol. 1, p. 590).

13. Mary Shelley to Walter Scott, 14 June 1818 (*Mary Shelley Letters*, vol. 1, pp. 71–2).

14. Godwin to Mary Shelley, 14 February 1823; MS. Abinger c. 46, fols 42–3.

15. *The Original Frankenstein*, ed. Charles E. Robinson (Oxford: Bodleian Library, 2008).

Chapter 6

1. Mary Shelley to Maria Gisborne, 15 August 1822 (*Mary Shelley Letters*, vol. 1, p. 245).

2. Journal of Edward Williams, 6 May 1822 (*Maria Gisborne & Edward E. Williams, Shelley's Friends: Their Journals and Letters*, ed. Frederick L. Jones (Norman: University of Oklahoma Press, 1951), p. 147).

3. *London Magazine* 9 (March 1824), pp. 253–6.

4. Mary Shelley to Maria Gisborne, *c.* 27 August 1822; MS. Shelley c. 1, fols 521–3 (*Mary Shelley Letters*, vol. 2, pp. 254–5).

5. MS. Shelley adds. c. 4, fol. 68.

6. Mary Shelley to Maria Gisborne, *c.* 27 August 1822; MS. Shelley c. 1, fols 521–3 (*Mary Shelley Letters*, vol. 2, pp. 254–5).

7. Mary Shelley to Jane Williams, 15 October 1822 (*Mary Shelley Letters*, vol. 1, pp. 280–83).

8. Mary Shelley to Maria Gisborne, 22 November 1822; MS Shelley c. 1, fols 531–2 (*Mary Shelley Letters*, vol. 1, pp. 290–93).

9. Mary Shelley to Jane Williams, 19 February 1823; MS. Abinger c. 46, fols 42–3 (*Mary Shelley Letters*, vol. 1, pp. 311–14).

10. (*The Journals of Mary Shelley 1814–1844*, ed. P.R. Feldman and D. Scott-Kilvert, 2 vols (Oxford, 1987)), pp. 440–41.

11. Journal entry, 11 November 1822 (*Mary Shelley Journals*, pp. 44).

12. MS. Shelley adds. c. 5, fol. 114.

13. Sir Timothy Shelley to Lord Byron, 8 February 1823; MS. Abinger c. 69, fols 2–3.

Chapter 7

1. Mary Shelley to Leigh Hunt, 9–11 September 1823; MS. Shelley adds. c. 6, fols 15–16 (*Mary Shelley Letters*, vol. 1, pp. 377–83).

2. Mary Shelley to Leigh Hunt, 18 September 1823; MS. Shelley adds. c. 6, fols 17–18 (*Mary Shelley Letters*, vol. 1, pp. 383–7).

3. Mary Shelley to Marianne Hunt, 27 November 1823; MS. Shelley adds. c. 6, fols 21–2 (*Mary Shelley Letters*, vol. 1, pp. 402–6).

4. Mary Shelley to Edward Moxon, 7 December 1838 (*Mary Shelley Letters*, vol. 2, pp. 300–301).

5. MS. Shelley adds. d. 6.

6. MS. Shelley adds. d. 7.

7. MS. Shelley adds. d. 8.

8. MS. Shelley adds. d. 9.

9. Thomas Love Peacock to William Whitton, 18 August 1824; MS. Shelley adds c. 8, fols 95-6 (*Letters of Thomas Love Peacock*, ed. Nicholas A. Joukovsky, 2 vols (Oxford: Clarendon Press, 2001), vol. 1, pp. 199-200.

10. Mary Shelley to John Bowring, 25 February 1826 (*Mary Shelley Letters*, vol. 1, pp. 512–13).

11. Mary Diana Dods to Mary Shelley, [1824–7]; MS. Abinger c. 47, fols 42–3.

12. Note, 9 May 1819; MS. Abinger c. 32, fol. 32.

13. Fragment; MS. Abinger c. 31, fol. 117.

14. Note, 30 June 1834; MS. Abinger c. 38, fol. 13.

15. Recent scholarly work on Godwin's private papers is nearing fruition: a catalogue of his papers has recently been published http://www.bodley. ox.ac.uk/dept/scwmss/wmss/online/1500-1900/abinger/abinger.html; an annotated online edition of his journal is under way; and an edition of his correspondence is forthcoming from Oxford University Press.

16. MS. Abinger c. 60, fol. 27r.

17. Mary Shelley to Edward Trelawny, 26 January 1837; MS. Shelley adds c. 6, fols 215–16 (*Mary Shelley Letters*, vol. 2, pp. 280–83).

18. Fanny Wright to Mary Shelley, 21 August 1827; MS. Abinger c. 47, fols 98–9.

19. Harriet de Boinville to Mary Shelley, 18 December 1837; MS. Abinger c. 49, fols 76–7.

20. Mary Shelley to Marianne Hunt, 10 October 1824; MS. Shelley adds c. 6, fols 31–2 (*Mary Shelley Letters*, vol. 1, p. 453).

21. Mary Shelley to John Cam Hobhouse, 10 November 1824 (*Mary Shelley Letters*, vol. 1, pp. 454–6).

22. Edward Trelawny to Mary Shelley, 11 March 1829; MS. Abinger c. 48, fols 45–6.

23. Mary Shelley to Edward Trelawny, April 1829 (*Mary Shelley Letters*, vol. 2, pp. 71–3).

24. Mary Shelley to Edward Trelawny, 27 July 1829; MS. Shelley adds. c. 6, fols 80–81 (*Mary Shelley Letters*, vol. 2, pp. 81–3).

25. Edward Trelawny to Mary Shelley, 20 October 1829; MS. Abinger c. 48, fols 57–8.

26. Mary Shelley to Edward Trelawny, 15 December 1829; MS. Shelley adds. c. 6, fols 86–7 (*Mary Shelley Letters*, vol. 2, pp. 93–6).

27. Mary Shelley to Edward Moxon, 11 November 1839 (*Mary Shelley Letters*, vol. 2, p. 330).

Chapter 8

1. Rolleston, *Talks with Lady Shelley*, pp. 30–31.

2. Quoted in R. Glynn Grylls, *Mary Shelley* (Oxford, 1938), p. 261.

3. Rolleston, *Talks with Lady Shelley*, pp. 102–3.

4. MS. Abinger c. 83, fol. 55.

5. Rolleston, *Talks with Lady Shelley*, pp. 64–5.

6. Mary Shelley to Rose Stewart, 1 May 1844 (*Mary Shelley Letters*, vol. 3, p. 131).

7. T.J. Hogg to Lady Shelley, 22 March 1857–15 March 1858; MS. Abinger c. 70, fols 10–34, 37–8, 42–8.

8. Mary Shelley to Marianne Hunt, 10 October 1824; MS. Shelley adds. c. 6, fols 31–2 (*Mary Shelley Letters*, vol. 1, pp. 451–4).

9. Lady Shelley to Sir Percy Shelley, [1858]; MS Abinger c. 74, fols 17–18.

10. Sir Percy Shelley to T.J. Hogg, 12 May 1858; MS Abinger c. 74, fols 111–12.

11. *Shelley Memorials*, p. 76.

12. Edward Trelawny to Lady Shelley, February 1857; MS. Abinger c. 70, fol. 58.

13. *Fraser's Magazine*, vol. 57 (June 1858), pp. 643–59.

14. *Fraser's Magazine*, vol. 61 (January 1860), pp. 91–109.

15. MS. Abinger c. 83, fol. 54.

16. Richard Garnett to Lady Shelley, 25 February 1872; MS. Abinger c. 70, fols 116–123.

17. Sir Percy Shelley to Richard Garnett, 1 September 1878; in *Letters about Shelley from the Richard Garnett Papers*, pp. 155–7.

18. Lady Shelley to Edward Trelawny, August 1878; MS. Abinger c. 73, fols 109–18.

19. Lady Shelley to Richard Garnett, 16 December 1878; in *Letters about Shelley from the Richard Garnett Papers*, pp. 157–8.

20. Sir Percy Shelley to ?Cartright, [n.d.]; MS. Abinger c. 74, fols 144–5.

21. Sir Henry Taylor to Edward Dowden, 7 July 1883; MS. Abinger c. 71, fols 32–3.

22. Rolleston, *Talks with Lady Shelley*, pp. 69–70.

23. Richard Garnett to Sir Percy Shelley, [1886]; MS. Abinger c. 82, fols 66–7.

24. William Michael Rossetti to Lady Shelley, 12 December 1889; MS. Abinger c. 72, fols 125–6.

25. Richard Garnett, 'Custody of the Shelley Papers'; MS. Abinger c. 83, fols 9–12.

26. Shelley to Thomas Love Peacock, 6 November 1818; MS. Shelley c. 1, fols 250–2 (*Shelley Letters*, vol. 2, pp. 45–48).

Chapter 9

1. Kenneth Neill Cameron, 'The Provenance of Shelley and His Circle Manuscripts', *Shelley and his Circle*, 4 vols (Cambridge MA: Harvard University Press, 1961–), vol. 2, p. 898.

2. Edwin Wolf 2nd and John F. Fleming, *Rosenbach: A Biography* (Cleveland and New York: World Publishers, 1960), p. 312.

3. Donald H. Reiman, 'The Four Ages of Editing and the English Romantics', *Text: Transactions of the Society for Textual Scholarship* 1, 1981, p. 236.

4. John Collins, *The Two Forgers: a Biography of Harry Buxton Forman and Thomas James Wise* (Aldershot: Scholar Press, 1992), p. 82.

5. Forman to Richard Maurice Bucke, November 1886, quoted in Collins, *The Two Forgers*, p. 78.

6. Quoted in Collins, *The Two Forgers*, p. 304, where he dates it *c.* 1913. The letter is held in the University of Kentucky Libraries.

7. Harry Buxton Forman to Thomas J. Wise, Forman's copy of the letter, Pforzheimer Collection, Shelleyana 21a, 1 September 1905.

8. Quoted in Cameron, ed. *Shelley and his Circle*, vol. 4, p. 512.

9. Collins, *The Two Forgers*, p. 206. He reports as his source Pip Newton of Quaritch's; however, the story was first told in almost the same words in Dwight Macdonald's *New Yorker* article of 10 November 1962, 'The First Editions of T.J. Wise', p. 193.

10. Wolf and Fleming, *Rosenbach*, pp. 312–13.

11. John Carter and Graham Pollard, *Enquiry into the Nature of Certain Nineteenth Century Pamphlets* (London: Constable; New York: Charles Scribner's Sons, both 1934).

12. Collins, *The Two Forgers*, pp. 272–3.

13. She and Shelley were married on 30 December 1816.

14. Taken from the Catalogue of the Scrope Davies Papers appended to T.A.J. Burnett, *The Rise and Fall of a Regency Dandy: The Life and Times of Scrope Berdmore Davies* (London: John Murray, 1981), pp. 239–43.

15. For much of the information in this section see Marion Kingston Stocking, 'Miss Tina and Miss Plin: The Papers behind *The Aspern Papers*', in Donald H. Reiman, Michael C. Jaye, and Betty T. Bennett, eds, *The Evidence of the Imagination: Studies of the Interactions between Life and Art in English Romantic Literature* (New York: New York University Press, 1978), pp. 372–84. Unpublished papers of Claire Clairmont in the Pforzheimer Collection also demonstrate her preoccupation.

16. Stocking, 'Miss Tina and Miss Plin', p. 375.

17. Ibid., p. 376.

18. Quoted in ibid., p. 377. ('Fundamentally, I was born to be a courtesan, though not brought up to the trade.')

19. Quoted from MSS. Houghton Library, Harvard University, BMS Am 1587 (22) in Marion Kingston Stocking, ed. *The Clairmont Correspondence: Letters of Claire Clairmont, Charles Clairmont, and Fanny Imlay Godwin*, vol. 2: *1835–1879* (Baltimore: Johns Hopkins University Press, 1995), Appendix C, p. 654.

20. *Manuscripts of the Younger Romantics*, vol. 5, *The Harvard Shelley Poetic Manuscripts…* ed. and intro. Donald H. Reiman (New York and London: Garland, 1991), p. xiii.

21. Reiman, Introduction to *The Harvard Shelley Poetic Manuscripts*, p. xvi.

22. Quoted in Stocking, *The Clairmont Correspondence*, vol. 2, Appendix D, p. 662.

23. Stocking, *The Clairmont Correspondence*, vol. 2, Appendix D, p. 663.

24. Donald H. Reiman, Introduction to *The Esdaile Notebook: A Facsimile of the Holograph Copybook*, ed. Donald H. Reiman (New York and London: Garland, 1985), p. xxi.

25. Kenneth Neill Cameron, Introduction to P.B. Shelley, *The Esdaile Notebook: A Volume of Early Poems* (New York: Alfred A. Knopf, 1964), p. 3.

26. Reiman, Introduction to *The Esdaile Notebook: A Facsimile*, p. xvi.

27. Ibid. pp. xx–xxi.

28. Carl H. Pforzheimer, Jr., Foreword to *The Esdaile Notebook: A Volume of Early Poems*, p. vii.

29. Doucet Devin Fischer, conversation, 27 April 2010.

30. Janice Williams, 'Bindings of Rare Books', undated, untitled, uncatalogued collection of essays in brown manila envelope addressed to the Pforzheimers from the Senior Class of the Lenox School; Pforzheimer Collection.

31. Stephen Wagner and Doucet Devin Fischer, *The Carl H. Pforzheimer Collection of Shelley and His Circle: A History, a Biography, and a Guide* (New York: New York Public Library, 1996), p. 12.

32. Donald H. Reiman, *Shelley and his Circle, 1773–1822*, vol. 5 (Cambridge MA: Cambridge University Press, 1973), p. 152.

33. Kenneth Neill Cameron, *Shelley and his Circle*, vol. 5, p. 142.

Further Reading

For a comprehensive and expert treatment of Shelley's notebooks and loose literary papers, with transcripts, facsimiles, bibliographical analyses and commentaries, see *The Bodleian Shelley Manuscripts*, ed. Donald H. Reiman, 23 vols (New York and London: Garland, 1986–2002).

For an appraisal of Shelley studies following the completion of the above edition, see *The Unfamiliar Shelley*, ed. Alan M. Weinberg and Timothy Webb (Farnham: Ashgate, 2009).

For an insightful and meticulous presentation of selected items from the Bodleian Shelley and Abinger collections, see B.C. Barker-Benfield, *Shelley's Guitar: An Exhibition of Manuscripts, First Editions and Relics, to Mark the Bicentenary of the Birth of Percy Bysshe Shelley, 1792–1992* (Oxford: Bodleian Library, 1992).

The recently completed catalogue of the Abinger Papers is available online at www.bodley.ox.ac.uk/dept/scwmss/wmss/online/1500-1900/abinger/abinger.html.

For the Abinger Papers, see also Pamela Clemit, 'William Godwin and James Watt's Copying Machine: Wet Transfer Copies in the Abinger Papers', *Bodleian Library Record*, vol. 18, no. 5 (2005), pp. 532–60; Pamela Clemit, 'William Godwin's Papers in the Abinger Deposit: An Unmapped Country', *Bodleian Library Record*, vol. 18, no. 3 (2004), pp. 253–63; William St. Clair, *The Godwins and the Shelleys: A Biography of a Family* (London: Faber & Faber, 1989).

For a facsimile edition of the Bodleian *Frankenstein* manuscripts, with transcripts and commentaries, see *Manuscripts of the Younger Romantics*, vol. IX: *The Frankenstein Notebooks*, ed. Charles E. Robinson, 2 vols (London and New York: Garland, 1996).

For a recent edition of *Frankenstein*, based on a new reading of the manuscripts, see *The Original Frankenstein*, ed. Charles E. Robinson (Oxford: Bodleian Library, 2008).

For Mary Shelley's editorial work on the family papers, see Paula R. Feldman, 'Biography and the Literary Executor: The Case of Mary W. Shelley', *The Papers of the Bibliographical Society of America*, vol. 73 (1978), pp. 287–97; Michael O'Neill, '"Trying to Make It as Good as I Can": Mary Shelley's Editing of Shelley's Poetry and Prose', *Mary Shelley in Her Times*, ed. Betty T. Bennett and Stuart Curran (Baltimore: Johns Hopkins University Press, 2000), pp. 185–97, 279–81; Susan J. Wolfson, 'Mary Shelley, Editor', in *The Cambridge Companion to Mary Shelley*, ed. Esther Schor (Cambridge: Cambridge University Press, 2003).

For Jane, Lady Shelley's activities as guardian of the papers, see Michael Rossington, 'Commemorating the Relic: The Beginnings of the Bodleian Shelley Collections', *Bodleian Library Record*, vol. 18, no. 3 (2004), pp. 264–75; Sylva Norman, *Flight of the Skylark: The Development of Shelley's Reputation* (Norman: University of Oklahoma Press, 1954); R. Glynn Grylls, *Mary Shelley: A Biography* (London and New York: Oxford University Press, 1938); Emily W. Sunstein, *Mary Shelley: Romance and Reality* (Boston: Little, Brown, 1989); Miranda Seymour, *Mary Shelley* (London: John Murray, 2000).

Index